Cliffsl

D0000260

Wilde's
The Importance of Being Earnest

By Susan Van Kirk

IN THIS BOOK

- Learn about the Life and Background of the Playwright
- Preview an Introduction to the Play
- Explore themes, literary devices, and use of dialog in the Critical Commentaries
- Examine in-depth Character Analyses
- Reinforce what you learn with CliffsNotes Review
- Find additional information to further your study in CliffsNotes Resource Center and online at www.cliffsnotes.com

WILEY

Wiley Publishing, Inc.

About the Author
Susan Van Kirk has taught high school English in Monmouth, Illinois, for 30 years.

Publisher's Acknowledgments
Editorial
Project Editor: Marcia L. Johnson
Acquisitions Editor: Greg Tubach
Copy Editor: Katie Robinson
Editorial Assistant: Amanda Harbin
Composition
Indexer: TECHBOOKS Production Services
Proofreader: TECHBOOKS Production Services
Wiley Indianapolis Composition Services

CliffsNotes™ *The Importance of Being Earnest*
Published by:
Wiley Publishing, Inc.
111 River St.
Hoboken, NJ 07030-5774
www.wiley.com

Copyright © 2004 Wiley Publishing, Inc. New York, New York
Library of Congress Cataloging-in-Publication Data is available from the Library of Congress.
ISBN: 0-7645-4461-6

10 9 8 7 6 5 4 3
1O/QZ/RS/QT/IN
Published by Wiley Publishing, Inc., New York, NY
Published simultaneously in Canada

WILEY

Table of Contents

How to Use This Book

This CliffsNotes study guide on Oscar Wilde's *The Importance of Being Earnest* supplements the original literary work, giving you background information about the author, an introduction to the work, a graphical character map, critical commentaries, expanded glossaries, and a comprehensive index, all for you to use as an educational tool that will allow you to better understand *The Importance of Being Earnest*. This study guide was written with the assumption that you have read *The Importance of Being Earnest*. Reading a literary work doesn't mean that you immediately grasp the major themes and devices used by the author; this study guide will help supplement your reading to be sure you get all you can from Wilde's *The Importance of Being Earnest*. CliffsNotes Review tests your comprehension of the original text and reinforces learning with questions and answers, practice projects, and more. For further information on Oscar Wilde and *The Importance of Being Earnest*, check out the Cliffs-Notes Resource Center.

CliffsNotes provides the following icons to highlight essential elements of particular interest:

Reveals the underlying themes in the work.

Helps you to more easily relate to or discover the depth of a character.

Uncovers elements such as setting, atmosphere, mystery, passion, violence, irony, symbolism, tragedy, foreshadowing, and satire.

Enables you to appreciate the nuances of words and phrases.

Don't Miss Our Web Site

Discover classic literature as well as modern-day treasures by visiting the CliffsNotes Web site at www.cliffsnotes.com. You can obtain a quick download of a Cliffs-Notes title, purchase a title in print form, browse our catalog, or view online samples.

You'll also find interactive tools that are fun and informative, links to interesting Web sites, tips, articles, and additional resources to help you, not only for literature, but for test prep, finance, careers, computers, and Internet, too. See you at www.cliffsnotes.com!

LIFE AND BACKGROUND OF THE PLAYWRIGHT

The following abbreviated biography of Oscar Wilde is provided so that you might become more familiar with his life and the historical times that possibly influenced his writing. Read this Life and Background of the Playwright section and recall it when reading Wilde's *The Importance of Being Earnest*, thinking of any thematic relationship between Wilde's play and his life.

Wilde's Early Years

Oscar Wilde's unconventional life began with an equally unconventional family. He was born Oscar Fingal O'Flahertie Wills Wilde on October 16, 1854, at 21 Westland Row, Dublin, Ireland. His father, Sir William Wilde, was an eminent Victorian and a doctor of aural surgery.

Wilde's mother, Jane Francesca Elgee (or Lady Wilde), saw herself as a revolutionary and liked to trace her family through the Italian line of Alighieris, including Dante. An Irish nationalist, she wrote under the pen name Speranza. She attracted artists like herself and established a literary salon devoted to intellectual and artistic conversations of the day, through which Lady Wilde brought literature, an interest in art and culture, and an elegance and appreciation for wit into the lives of her children.

Wilde had two siblings: an older brother named Willie, born in 1852, and a sister, Isola, born in 1856, but who died at the age of 10. These offspring would not experience a standard, conventional childhood. Through their home passed intellectuals, artists, and internationally known doctors—and the children were not left to a governess or nanny. Allowed to mingle and eat with the guests, they learned to value intellectual and witty conversation, an influence that would have profound and long-lasting effects on young Oscar Wilde.

Education, Travel, and Celebrity

Wilde was given the advantage of a superior education. At age 11, he entered the exclusive Portora Royal School and began to assert the scholarship and intellect that would bring him both great celebrity and great sadness. His long interest in all things Greek began at Portora. Winning several prizes, he was already a first-rate classics scholar and ready to pursue serious studies.

Wilde went on to Trinity College where he extended his interest in the classics and his long list of intellectual accomplishments. He won an additional scholarship, made first class in examinations, received a composition prize for Greek verse, and the Berkeley Gold Medal for Greek. In 1874 he received a scholarship to Magdalen College in Oxford. His lifelong love of the classics would continue through his university career and immensely influence his subsequent writing. Little did he know what turns and twists his life would take when he entered Oxford and came under the influence of three very powerful professors.

Wilde's four years at Oxford (1874–1878) were dizzy, personality-changing times. By graduation he was firmly committed to the pursuit of pleasure and the careful devising of a public persona, which included unconventional clothing and the pose of a dandy. Wilde's direction in life changed because of the influence of three professors—Ruskin, Pater, and Mahaffy.

The magnetism of Professor John Ruskin, author of *Modern Painters* and *The Stones of Venice,* attracted Wilde's imagination. Ruskin believed civilizations could be judged by their art, which must consider and reflect moral values. Ruskin also stirred Wilde's aristocratic soul with social concerns in his insistence that his students identify with the working class and do manual labor. His influence on Wilde's social conscience is undeniable, and it permeates Wilde's plays and his essay, "The Soul of Man Under Socialism." Wilde did not, however, agree with Ruskin on the moral purposes of art. Influenced by Keats and his ideas of truth and beauty, he believed art should be loved and appreciated for its own sake.

Yet another Oxford influence was Professor Walter Pater, author of *Studies in the History of the Renaissance* and *Marius the Epicurian.* His prose style influenced young Wilde, and his ideas seemed to fit Wilde's new-found proclivities. Pater emphasized art for art's sake and urged his students to live with passion and for sensual pleasure, testing new ideas and not conforming to the orthodoxy. Pater was planting seeds in fertile ground. The Aesthetic Movement, an avant-garde philosophy of the 1870s, was in full bloom, and its advocates were critical of the heavy, moralistic Victorian taste. They wanted to pursue forms of beauty in opposition to the art and architecture of the day. Wilde could not agree more. He went overboard into aesthetics, adopting extravagant clothing styles, which continued when he left Oxford for London in 1878. He thought of himself as an aesthete, poet, writer, and nonconformist—and he wanted to be famous or at least infamous.

A third influence on Wilde at Oxford was Mahaffy, an Oxford professor of ancient history. Professor Mahaffy took him along on trips to Italy and Greece.

By 1878, when Wilde completed his degree at Oxford, he had won the coveted Newdigate Prize for his poem "Ravenna." Leaving Oxford, Wilde was now ready to take on the world with a classical education and an unequivocal inclination toward the unconventional. Wilde proved to be a master of public relations. Virtually unknown and unpublished, he single-handedly created his own celebrity. While his travels and lectures increased his fame both in England and abroad, his early writings were not critical successes.

London in the 1870s provided Wilde the opportunity to build a public persona and test the limits of what society would tolerate. He dressed in strange clothes and often sported flowers such as lilies and sunflowers. He built a reputation as a minor luminary by courting celebrities. In 1880, he privately printed his first play, *Vera,* and the following year published his first book of poems. The poems were a modest success, but the play died a quick death.

In April 1881, Gilbert and Sullivan opened a play titled *Patience* in which a primary character, Bunthorne, was assumed to be based on Wilde. This false assumption was promoted by Wilde through early attendance—in outrageous clothes—at the play. When the play moved on to New York in December 1881, Richard D'Oyly Carte, the producer, hired Wilde to do a series of lectures to introduce the play to American audiences. The press was alerted and ready for his arrival, and Wilde played to them by proclaiming at customs that he had nothing to declare but his genius.

What began as a modest tour ripened into a six-month nationwide tour. He spoke in New York, Chicago, Boston, Fort Wayne (Indiana), Omaha (Nebraska), Philadelphia, and Washington. He even lectured in the mining town of Leadville, Colorado, where his ability to hold his liquor brought him a silver drill and the good-humored admiration of the miners. America seemed intrigued by Wilde's odd character, and he, in turn, admired many things American, including the democratic insistence on universal education. While in America, Wilde's lectures included "The English Renaissance of Art," "The House Beautiful," and "Decorative Art in America." As a celebrity, he dined with Henry Wadsworth Longfellow, Oliver Wendell Holmes, Charles Eliot Norton (the famous Harvard professor), and Walt Whitman. He also had audiences with Lincoln's son, Robert, and Jefferson Davis.

Following his triumphant tour, Wilde had enough money to spend three months in Paris. There he finished a forgettable play titled *The Duchess of Padua.* He was befriended once again by celebrities; this time they were Europeans: Zola, Hugo, Verlaine, Gide, Toulouse-Lautrec, Degas, and Pissarro. Obviously, early training at his mother's salon had paid off.

He returned to London looking for backers to produce his play. In an attempt to garner backing, he cut his hair short and dressed more conservatively. When he was unsuccessful in finding producers, he arranged for a production in New York for $1,000. The play was not successful, closing in less than a week. So, Wilde went back to England, arranging a lecture tour of Great Britain and Ireland, where he encountered a previous acquaintance, Constance Lloyd, who would become his wife—for better or for worse.

Marriage and Commercial Success

During the seven years between his wedding to Constance and his first introduction to a young man who would become part of his downfall—Lord Alfred Douglas—Wilde settled down to a life of domestic respectability as a husband and father. By all accounts the Wildes' marriage was happy, producing two sons: Cyril in June 1885 and Vyvyan in November 1886. Wilde played often with his children and loved them immensely. To support them he wrote book reviews for newspapers and magazines, including the *Pall Mall Gazette* and the *Dramatic Review.* Occasionally, he lectured. *The Lady's World* magazine named him its editor in 1887, and he converted it from a fashion magazine to *The Woman's World* with essays about women's viewpoints on art, music, literature, and modern life. He wrote essays that took women seriously as creative and intelligent human beings. When he was an editor, Wilde's life was financially more secure. In 1888 he wrote a book of fairy tales titled *The Happy Prince and Other Tales,* and in 1889 he wrote an essay titled "The Decay of Lying." He left the magazine in July 1889 to begin his greatest period of playwriting.

A Playwright with a Secret Life

Within six months of leaving *The Woman's World,* Wilde had published the commercially successful novel, *The Picture of Dorian Gray,* about a man with a secret life. This novel was quickly followed by *Intentions, Lord Arthur Savile's Crime and Other Stories,* and *A House of Pomegranates.* In the period from 1891 to 1892, he produced *Salome, Lady Windermere's Fan, A Woman of No Importance,* and an essay, "The Soul of Man Under Socialism." He amused his audiences, and in return they offered standing ovations at his plays.

One would think all this good luck, publicity, and commercial success would be enough for a respectable married man with two sons, who finally was receiving acceptance from British aristocracy. However, during this amazingly prolific period, Wilde was beginning to frequent literary circles that were often homosexual. In 1886, he is said to have had his first homosexual affair with a Canadian named Robert Ross. He was also introduced to Alfred Taylor, who lived in Bloomsbury and often had male prostitutes at his home. One of these young men was the unemployed Charles Parker. Wilde became involved with several of these young men, who later testified against him at trial.

In 1891, Oscar Wilde met the young man who would change his life forever. Lord Alfred Douglas (known as Bosie) was the 21-year-old son of the Marquis of Queensberry. A very controversial figure, Douglas was often described as femininely beautiful, aristocratic, rich, homosexual, and poetic. His hold on Wilde has often been a subject of conjecture, but most writers believe that Wilde, 14 years Bosie's senior, was infatuated, obsessed, and besotted. By 1892, the two were together constantly. They traveled to France, Italy, and Algiers. Wilde rented homes for them outside London, and when they were apart he wrote letters and was careless with their whereabouts.

Wilde enjoyed unprecedented success in the London theatres from 1893 to 1895. He had two plays running simultaneously in the West End: *A Woman of No Importance* opened at the Royal Theatre, Haymarket, in January 1893, and *Lady Windermere's Fan* began in November of that same year. From August through September 1894, he wrote *The Importance of Being Earnest* at the seaside resort of Worthing, Sussex, his wife and children enjoying the holiday with him. By 1895, he had the acclaim of all London for his witty society plays. However, he was also increasingly indiscreet about his personal life. The year 1895 marked the beginning of the end of his public acceptance and the privacy of his secret life.

Disaster and Ruin

Rumors about Wilde's secret life were already circulating in 1895, but he was still very amusing, and as long as his indiscretions were kept quiet, society did not care. *The Importance of Being Earnest* opened on February 14 at St. James' Theatre, beginning a run of 86 performances to standing ovations. On February 28, the Marquis of Queensberry left a card for Wilde at his club, the Albemarle Club. It read: "To Oscar Wilde, posing as a sodomite." (Actually, sodomite was misspelled.) Estranged from his father and hating him, Douglas encouraged Wilde to sue the Marquis for libel. Convinced he could triumph in court, Wilde declared to his lawyers that he was innocent and wanted to press the lawsuit. His friends, knowing he had been too indiscreet, urged him to go abroad with his wife until it all blew over, but Wilde intended to carry through with the case. The Marquis hired detectives and, using Alfred Taylor and his young prostitutes, Queensberry effectively put Wilde on trial for homosexuality.

The libel trial was disastrous. When the prosecution threatened to bring in male prostitutes to testify, Wilde dropped the case and left in disgrace. But tragedy was not over for Oscar Wilde. In 1885, Parliament had passed the Criminal Law Amendment Act. It was used to try acts of "gross indecency" between men and sometimes could result in hanging. Being a homosexual was not a crime; the sexual act itself was. When the first trial ended, Queensberry's lawyers sent a transcript of the trial to public prosecutors. Home Secretary Herbert Asquith decided to arrest, imprison, and try Wilde, but he delayed the warrant long enough for Wilde to leave on the last boat-train to France. Wilde, for various reasons, remained in England and was arrested. A new trial would take place, indicting Wilde.

The press had a heyday, viciously attacking Wilde and holding up Queensberry—hardly a model citizen. They pictured Wilde as a deviant but could not print the crime with which he was charged. Unflattering cartoons and caricatures appeared in magazines such as *Punch,* and Wilde was pictured in unmanly clothes with flowers in his lapel. The court found Wilde guilty and sentenced him to two years at hard labor.

Today, transcripts of the trials can be read in H. Montgomery Hyde's *The Trials of Oscar Wilde* (The Notable Trials Library by Gryphon Editions, Inc., 1989). Just as Wilde's plays noted the huge gulf between the rich and the working class, the trials themselves displayed the disparity. Lord Alfred Douglas, protected by his powerful family name, was never charged, even though the jury inquired about this because he had committed the same crime. The names of upper-class people associated with the case could not be mentioned in court; in fact, some witnesses were instructed to write a name rather than say it aloud. The names of working class people, however, were readily identified aloud.

The immediate aftermath of the trial was a total disgrace for Wilde. He was abandoned by his friends, his book sales ended, his plays were closed down, and his belongings were sold at auction at low prices. He began his sentence in Newgate Prison but was moved to different prisons over the next two years.

Oscar Wilde was not a man well equipped to face such solitary adversity. His world was normally one of social calendars and lots of people. He was moved to Pentonville Prison where he spent 23 hours a day in poorly ventilated cells and 1 hour exercising without speaking to anyone. His cell was unsanitary, and his bed was nothing more than wooden boards. The food was unspeakable, and he could only read the *Bible,* a prayer book, and a hymn book. Wilde was not allowed photos of his wife or children or allowed to write or receive more than one letter in three months. In February 1896, his mother dying, Wilde requested leave to go to her. His request was denied; Constance visited the prison on February 19 to tell him in person of his mother's death. It was their last meeting.

By now Wilde had lost 30 pounds, and was not doing well physically or emotionally. He was transferred to Wandsworth Prison. A parliamentary committee looking into prison conditions took up his case and, because he was destitute, transferred him to Reading Gaol—a debtors' prison—for the remainder of his time. While he was there, Wilde wrote a famous letter to Douglas justifying his life and position, which was later published as "De Profundis." When he left this prison on May 19, 1897, he was in decent health and departed immediately for France, never to return to England.

Wilde's Last Years

Wilde's last years were spent in several towns in Europe. He settled in the small village of Berneval-sur-Mer near Dieppe, France, and sent letters to newspapers on prison reform while writing his greatest poem, "The Ballad of Reading Gaol." His wife Constance had settled in Italy with the boys, changing their name to Holland because of the scandal. Wilde wanted to see her and the children, but she refused because he would not give up Douglas. He and Bosie reunited, and Constance died in April 1898. There was no more writing; Wilde drank heavily and begged money from friends. He and Bosie moved to Naples, Switzerland, and Paris, but Wilde's health was fading. During his time in prison, he had found an admiration for Jesus Christ and had written about his religious convictions. Just prior to his death in Paris on November 30, 1900, at the age of 46, Wilde converted to Roman Catholicism.

Over the last century and a half, many people have believed that Wilde died of cerebral meningitis, complicated by syphilis, and many have seen it as proof of his depravity. However, a November 2000 article in the British journal, *Lancet,* blames meningoencephalitis, complicated by a chronic right middle-ear disease (see Resource Center for the article). Wilde was treated before and during his imprisonment for a chronic ear infection. Surgery for an acute and life-threatening infection, which had moved into the mastoid, was allegedly performed on October 10, 1900, and was documented in Wilde's letters. He suffered a relapse in November of that year and fell into a coma, never to awaken. His son, Vyvyan, ironically underwent a similar operation for mastoid infection less than two months after his father died.

Wilde's death did not end the public's appreciation of his marvelous wit and staging. *The Importance of Being Earnest* returned to the West End with revivals in 1902, 1909, 1911, and 1913. The original producer, George Alexander, willed the copyright of the play to Wilde's son, Vyvyan.

After Wilde's death, many friends and acquaintances destroyed his letters for fear that their own reputations would be tainted by his scandal. Even letters to Constance during his imprisonment were destroyed. Most popular and academic writing about Wilde, since his death, has been about the scandal and speculation concerning his private life. His writing was largely ignored or devalued until the 1960s and 1970s. Now Wilde is often classified as a literary figure whose sensibilities, witticisms, and theatrical staging reflected the social commentary of the nineteenth century and influenced the theatre of the twentieth century.

INTRODUCTION TO THE PLAY

The following Introduction section is provided solely as an educational tool and is not meant to replace the experience of your reading the play. Read the Introduction and Brief Synopsis to enhance your understanding of the play and to prepare yourself for the critical thinking that should take place whenever you read any literary work. Keep the List of Characters and Character Map at hand so that as you read the original play, if you encounter a character about whom you're uncertain, you can refer to the List of Characters and Character Map to refresh your memory.

Introduction

The Importance of Being Earnest opened in the West End of London in February 1894 during an era when many of the religious, social, political, and economic structures were experiencing change—The Victorian Age (the last 25–30 years of the 1800s). The British Empire was at its height and occupied much of the globe, including Ireland, Wilde's homeland. The English aristocracy was dominant, snobbish and rich—far removed from the British middle class and poor.

Many novelists, essayists, poets, philosophers, and playwrights of the Victorian Age wrote about social problems, particularly concerning the effects of the Industrial Revolution and political and social reform. Dickens concentrated on the poor, Darwin wrote his theory of evolution describing the survival of the fittest, and Thomas Hardy wrote about the Naturalist Theory of man stuck in the throes of fate. Other notable writers such as Thackeray, the Brontes, Swinburne, Butler, Pinero, and Kipling were also contemporaries of Oscar Wilde. In an age of change, their work, as well as Wilde's plays, encouraged people to think about the artificial barriers that defined society and enabled a privileged life for the rich at the expense of the working class.

American writer, Edith Wharton, was also writing about the lifestyles of the rich during the same period. Her novels, such as Ethan Frome, The Age of Innocence, or The House of Mirth, explore the concepts of wealth and privilege at the expense of the working class on the American side of the Atlantic.

Although the themes in The Importance of Being Earnest address Victorian social issues, the structure of the play was largely influenced by French theatre, melodrama, social drama, and farce. Wilde was quite familiar with these genres, and borrowed from them freely. A play by W. Lestocq and E.M. Robson, The Foundling, is thought to be a source of Earnest, and it was playing in London at the time Wilde was writing Earnest. The Foundling has an orphan-hero, like Jack Worthing in Wilde's play. A farce is a humorous play using exaggerated physical action, such as slapstick, absurdity, and improbability. It often contains surprises where the unexpected is disclosed. The ending of Earnest, in which Jack misidentifies Prism as his unmarried mother, is typical of the endings of farces. Farces were usually done in three acts and often included changes of identity, stock characters, and lovers misunderstanding each other. Wearing mourning clothes or gobbling food down at times of stress are conventions that can be traced to early farces.

Norwegian playwright, Henrik Ibsen also strongly influenced Wilde. Ibsen's innovations in *A Doll's House,* which had played in London in 1889, were known to Wilde. Wilde also attended *Hedda Gabler* and *Ghosts,* two other plays by Ibsen. While in prison, Wilde requested copies of Ibsen plays.

The theatre manager of the St. James where *Earnest* opened, George Alexander, asked Wilde to reduce his original four-act play to three acts, like more conventional farces. Wilde accomplished this by omitting the Gribsby episode and merging two acts into one. In doing so, he maneuvered his play for greater commercial and literary response. (Visit www.cliffsnotes.com for commentary on the Gribsby episode.)

Marriage plots and social comedy were also typical of 1890s literature. Jane Austen and George Eliot were both novelists who used the idea of marriage as the basis for their conflicts. Many of the comedies of the stage were social comedies, plays set in contemporary times discussing current problems. The white, Anglo-Saxon, male society of the time provided many targets of complacency and aristocratic attitudes that playwrights such as Wilde could attack.

Earnest came at a time in Wilde's life when he was feeling the pressure of supporting his family and mother, and precariously balancing homosexual affairs—especially with Lord Alfred Douglas. *The Importance of Being Earnest* opened at George Alexander's St. James Theatre on February 14, 1895. On this particular evening, to honor Wilde's aestheticism, the women wore lily corsages, and the young men wore lilies of the valley in their lapels. Wilde himself, an outside observer by birth in the world of elegant fashion, was festooned in a glittering outfit. It was widely reported that he wore a coat with a black velvet collar, a white waistcoat, a black moiré ribbon watch chain with seals, white gloves, a green scarab ring, and lilies of the valley in his lapel. Wilde, the Irish outsider, was dramatically accepted by upper-class London, who loved his wit and daring, even when laughing about themselves.

The aristocracy attending Wilde's play knew and understood the private lives of characters like Jack and Algernon. They were aware of the culture and atmosphere of the West End. It had clubs, hotels, cafes, restaurants, casinos, and most of the 50 theatres in London. The West End was also a red-light district filled with brothels that could provide any pleasure. It was a virtual garden of delights, and the patrons could understand the need for married men to invent Ernests and Bunburys so that they could frolic in this world.

Brief Synopsis

The play begins in the flat of wealthy Algernon Moncrieff (Algy) in London's fashionable West End. Algernon's aunt (Lady Bracknell) and her daughter (Gwendolen Fairfax) are coming for a visit, but Mr. Jack Worthing (a friend of Algy's) arrives first. Algernon finds it curious that Jack has announced himself as "Ernest." When Jack explains that he plans to propose marriage to Gwendolen, Algy demands to know why Jack has a cigarette case with the inscription, "From little Cecily with her fondest love." Jack explains that his real name is Jack Worthing, squire, in the country, but he assumes the name "Ernest" when he ventures to the city for fun. Cecily is his ward. While devouring all the cucumber sandwiches, Algernon confesses that he, too, employs deception when it's convenient. He visits an imaginary invalid friend named Bunbury when he needs an excuse to leave the city.

Lady Bracknell and Gwendolen arrive. Algernon explains that he cannot attend Lady Bracknell's reception because he must visit his invalid friend, Bunbury, but he offers to arrange the music for her party. While Algernon distracts Lady Bracknell in another room, Jack proposes to Gwendolen. Unfortunately, she explains that she really wants to marry someone named Ernest because it sounds so solidly aristocratic. However, she accepts his proposal, and he makes a mental note to be rechristened Ernest. Lady Bracknell returns and refutes the engagement. She interrogates Jack and finds him lacking in social status. On her way out, Lady Bracknell tells Jack that he must find some acceptable parents. Gwendolen returns for Jack's address in the country. Algernon overhears and writes the address on his shirt cuff. He is curious about Cecily and decides to go "bunburying" in the country.

In the second act, the scene shifts to Jack Worthing's country estate where Miss Prism, Cecily Cardew's governess, is teaching Cecily in the garden. Miss Prism sings Jack's praises as a sensible and responsible man, unlike his brother Ernest, who is wicked and has a weak character. She teaches Cecily that good people end happily, and bad people end unhappily, according to the romantic novel Miss Prism wrote when she was young. The local vicar, Canon Chasuble, arrives and, sensing an opportunity for romance, takes Miss Prism for a walk in the garden. While they are gone, Algy shows up pretending to be Jack's wicked brother Ernest. He is overcome by Cecily's beauty. Determined to learn more about Cecily while Jack is absent, Algernon plans to stay for the weekend, then make a fast getaway before Jack arrives on Monday. However, Jack returns early in mourning clothes claiming that his brother Ernest has died in Paris. He is shocked to find Algy there posing as Ernest. He orders a dogcart—a small horse-drawn carriage—to send Algy back to London, but it is too late. Algernon is in love with Cecily and plans to stay there. When Jack goes out, Algernon proposes to Cecily, who gets out a diary and letters that she has already written, explaining that she had already imagined their engagement. She has always wanted to marry someone named Ernest, so Algy, like Jack, needs to arrange a rechristening.

Just when it seems that Jack and Algernon couldn't get into worse trouble, Gwendolen arrives, pursuing Jack, and discovers that his ward, Cecily, is unpleasantly beautiful. In conversation, they discover that they are both engaged to Ernest Worthing. A battle follows, cleverly carried out during the British tea ceremony. The situation is tense. Jack and Algernon arrive, and, in attempting to straighten out the Ernest problem, they alienate both women. The two men follow, explaining that they are going to be rechristened Ernest, and the women relent and agree to stay engaged.

Lady Bracknell shows up demanding an explanation for the couples' plans. When she discovers the extent of Cecily's fortune, she gives her consent to her engagement to Algernon; however, Jack's parentage is still a stumbling block to her blessings. Jack tells Lady Bracknell that he will not agree to Cecily's engagement until she is of age (35) unless he can marry Gwendolen. Dr. Chasuble arrives and announces that all is ready for the christenings. Jack explains that the christenings will no longer be necessary. Noting that Jack's present concerns are secular, the minister states that he will return to the church where Miss Prism is waiting to see him. Shocked at hearing the name "Prism," Lady Bracknell immediately calls for Prism and reveals her as the governess who lost Lady Bracknell's nephew 28 years earlier on a walk with the baby carriage. She demands to know where the baby is. Miss Prism explains that in a moment of distraction she placed the baby in her handbag and left him in Victoria Station, confusing him with her three-volume novel, which was placed in the baby carriage. After Jack asks for details, he quickly runs to his room and retrieves the handbag. Miss Prism identifies it, and Lady Bracknell reveals that Jack is Algernon's older brother, son of Ernest John Moncrieff, who died years ago in India. Jack now truly is Ernest, and Algernon/Cecily, Jack/Gwendolen, and Chasuble/Prism fall into each others' arms as Jack realizes the importance of being earnest.

List of Characters

John (Jack) Worthing   A young, eligible bachelor about town. In the city he goes by the name Ernest, and in the country he is Jack—a local magistrate of the county with responsibilities. His family pedigree is a mystery, but his seriousness and sincerity are evident. He proposes to The Honorable Gwendolen Fairfax and, though leading a double life, eventually demonstrates his conformity to the Victorian moral and social standards.

Algernon Moncrieff   A languid poser of the leisure class, bored by conventions and looking for excitement. He, too, leads a double life, being Algernon in the city and Ernest in the country. Algernon, unlike Jack, is not serious and is generally out for his own gratification. He falls in love and proposes to Jack's ward, Cecily, while posing as Jack's wicked younger brother, Ernest.

Lady Bracknell   The perfect symbol of Victorian earnestness—the belief that style is more important than substance and that social and class barriers are to be enforced. Lady Bracknell is Algernon's aunt trying to find a suitable wife for him. A strongly opinionated matriarch, dowager, and tyrant, she believes wealth is more important than breeding and bullies everyone in her path. Ironically, she married into the upper class from beneath it. She attempts to bully her daughter, Gwendolen.

The Honorable Gwendolen Fairfax   Lady Bracknell's daughter, exhibiting some of the sophistication and confidence of a London socialite, believes style to be important, not sincerity. She is submissive to her mother in public but rebels in private. While demonstrating the absurdity of such ideals as only marrying a man named Ernest, she also agrees to marry Jack despite her mother's disapproval of his origins.

Cecily Cardew   Jack Worthing's ward, daughter of his adopted father, Sir Thomas Cardew. She is of debutante age, 18, but she is being tutored at Jack's secluded country estate by Miss Prism, her governess. She is romantic and imaginative, and feeling the repression of Prism's rules. A silly and naïve girl, she declares that she wants to meet a "wicked man." Less sophisticated than Gwendolen, she falls in love with Algernon but feels he would be more stable if named Ernest.

Miss Prism   Cecily's governess and a symbol of Victorian moral righteousness. She is educating Cecily to have no imagination or sensationalism in her life. Quoting scripture as a symbol of her Victorian morality, she reveals a secret life of passion by her concern for the whereabouts of her misplaced novel and her flirtation with the local vicar. She becomes the source of Jack's revelation about his parents.

Rev. Canon Chasuble, D.D.   Like Miss Prism, he is the source of Victorian moral judgments, but under the surface he appears to be an old lecher. His sermons are interchangeable, mocking religious conventions. Like the servants, he does what Jack (the landowner) wants: performing weddings, christenings, sermons, funerals, and so on. However, beneath the religious exterior, his heart beats for Miss Prism.

Lane and Merriman   Servants of Algernon and Jack. Lane says soothing and comforting things to his employer but stays within the neutral guidelines of a servant. He is leading a double life, eating sandwiches and drinking champagne when his master is not present. He aids and abets the lies of Algernon. Merriman keeps the structure of the plot working: He announces people and happenings. Like Lane, he does not comment on his "betters," but solemnly watches their folly. His neutral facial expressions during crisis and chaos undoubtedly made the upper-class audience laugh.

Character Map

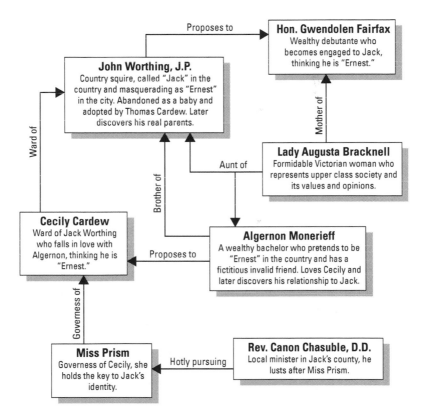

Proposes to

Hon. Gwendolen Fairfax
Wealthy debutante who becomes engaged to Jack, thinking he is "Ernest."

John Worthing, J.P.
Country squire, called "Jack" in the country and masquerading as "Ernest" in the city. Abandoned as a baby and adopted by Thomas Cardew. Later discovers his real parents.

Mother of

Ward of

Lady Augusta Bracknell
Formidable Victorian woman who represents upper class society and its values and opinions.

Aunt of

Brother of

Cecily Cardew
Ward of Jack Worthing who falls in love with Algernon, thinking he is "Ernest."

Proposes to

Algernon Moncrieff
A wealthy bachelor who pretends to be "Ernest" in the country and has a fictitious invalid friend. Loves Cecily and later discovers his relationship to Jack.

Governess of

Miss Prism
Governess of Cecily, she holds the key to Jack's identity.

Hotly pursuing

Rev. Canon Chasuble, D.D.
Local minister in Jack's county, he lusts after Miss Prism.

CRITICAL COMMENTARIES

The sections that follow provide great tools for supplementing your reading of *The Importance of Being Earnest*. First, in order to enhance your understanding of and enjoyment from reading, we provide quick summaries in case you have difficulty when you read the original literary work. Each summary is followed by commentary: literary devices, character analyses, themes, and so on. Keep in mind that the interpretations here are solely those of the author of this study guide and are used to jumpstart your thinking about the work. No single interpretation of a complex work like *The Importance of Being Earnest* is infallible or exhaustive, and you'll likely find that you interpret portions of the work differently from the author of this study guide. Read the original work and determine your own interpretations, referring to these Notes for supplemental meanings only.

Act I—Part 1

Summary

The curtain opens on the flat of wealthy Algernon Moncrieff in London's fashionable West End. While Algernon (Algy, for short) plays the piano, his servant (Lane) is arranging cucumber sandwiches for the impending arrival of Algernon's aunt (Lady Bracknell) and her daughter (Gwendolen). Mr. Jack Worthing (a friend of Moncrieff's and known to him as Ernest) arrives first. Jack announces that he plans to propose marriage to Gwendolen, but Algernon claims that he will not consent to their marriage until Jack explains why he is known as Ernest and why he has a cigarette case with a questionable inscription from a mysterious lady.

Jack claims that he has made up the character of Ernest because it gives him an excuse to visit the city. In the country, however, he is known as Jack Worthing, squire, with a troubled brother named Ernest. At first he lies and says the cigarette case is from his Aunt Cecily. Algernon calls his bluff, and Jack confesses that he was adopted by Mr. Thomas Cardew when he was a baby and that he is a guardian to Cardew's granddaughter, Cecily, who lives on his country estate with her governess, Miss Prism.

Similarly, Algernon confesses that he has invented an imaginary invalid friend, named Bunbury, whom he visits in the country when he feels the need to leave the city. After speculating on marriage and the need to have an excuse to get away, the two agree to dine together at the fashionable Willis', and Jack enlists Algernon's assistance in distracting Lady Bracknell so that Jack can propose to Gwendolen.

Commentary

Literary Device

Wilde sets the tone for hilarious mischief in this first scene. The many layers of meaning work together to entertain and to provoke thought. He makes fun of all the Victorians hold sacred, but in a light-hearted, amusing wordfest. His humor has multiple layers of meaning: social criticism of the upper and middle Victorian class values, references to the homosexual community and its culture, use of locales and landmarks familiar to his upper-class audience, and epigrams—short, witty sayings—and puns that not only provide humor but also reinforce his social critique.

First, Wilde must introduce his characters and setting. Both Jack and Algernon are living their lives through masks; deliberately, their double lives parallel Wilde's living as a married man with a clandestine homosexual life. Both characters are also recognizable to the upper- and middle-class audiences as stock figures.

Character Insight

Algernon is a stylish dandy—a young man very concerned about his clothes and appearance—in the pose of the leisure-class man about town. His fashionable apartment in a stylish locale immediately tells the audience that they are watching a comedy about the upper class. After introducing Algernon, Wilde turns him into a comic figure of self-gratification, stuffing his mouth with cucumber sandwiches. Self-gratification is ammunition against the repressive Victorian values of duty and virtue. In fact, as Algernon and Jack discuss marriage and Gwendolen, food becomes a symbol for lust, a topic not discussed in polite society. Much of what Algernon says is hopeless triviality, beginning a motif that Wilde will follow throughout the play: Society never cares about substance but instead reveres style and triviality. Wilde seems to be saying that in Victorian society people seem unaware of the difference between trivial subjects and the more valuable affairs of life.

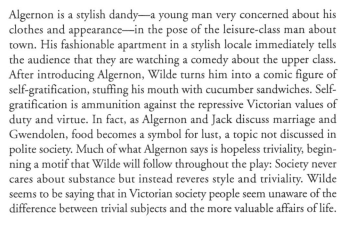
Character Insight

Jack is a little more serious than Algernon, perhaps because of his position as a country magistrate and his concern over his unconventional lineage. Helplessly a product of his time and social standing, Jack knows the rules, the appropriate manners, and the virtue of turning a phrase beautifully. He is an accepted upper-class gentleman, mainly because of the Cardew fortune. Novels written during this period, such as those of Charles Dickens, often turned on melodramatic plot devices such as the orphan discovering his real identity and winning his true love. Wilde hilariously turns this popular orphan plot on its head by having Jack found in a handbag in a major railroad station. Absurdity is Wilde's forte.

Both men are living a secret life, Jack with his Ernest identity and Algernon with his friend, Bunbury. Even Lane, Algy's servant, seems to have a second life in which he filches champagne and sandwiches from his "betters." Wilde seems to be saying that in a society where all is respectable but dull, a fictitious identity is necessary to liven things up. The classic nineteenth-century farce often turned on such mix-ups.

Theme

The deliberate use of the name Ernest is calculated. Earnestness, or devotion to virtue and duty, was a Victorian ideal. It stood for sincerity, seriousness, and hard work. Duty to one's family and name was a form of earnestness. Wilde turns these connotations upside down, making Ernest a name used for deception. Some critics suggest that *earnest* (in this context) means a double life. Other critics believe that *earnest* is understood in some circles to mean homosexual. By using the name Ernest throughout the play, and even in the title, Wilde is making references to social criticism, his own life, and his plot devices. He playfully makes a pun using *earnest/Ernest* when Algernon says, "You are the most earnest-looking person I ever saw in my life," following his discussion of Ernest as Jack's name.

Theme

Marriage in Victorian England comes under fire throughout the first act. Wilde saw marriages filled with hypocrisy and often used to achieve status. Wilde also saw marriage as an institution that encouraged cheating and snuffed out sexual attraction between spouses. When Lane says that wine is never of superior quality in a married household, Algernon questions Lane's marital status. Lane flippantly mentions that his own marriage resulted from a "misunderstanding." The nonsense continues as Jack explains that his purpose in coming to the city was to propose. Algernon replies that he thought Jack had "come up for pleasure? . . . I call that business." Algernon humorously explains that to be in love is romantic, but a proposal is never romantic because "one may be accepted." Marriage brings about an end to the romantic excitement of flirting: ". . . girls never marry the men they flirt with. Girls don't think it right." Each of these references to marriage or courtship trivializes a serious subject and turns around accepted values. Wilde corrupts the maxim, "Two's company; three's a crowd," to humorously chide the conservative audience. Algernon says, "In married life three is company and two is none." So much for the joys of wedded life. In short, Wilde seems to say that marriage is a business deal containing property, wealth, and status. Family names and bloodlines are deathly important.

Literary Device

Wilde uses food and eating as symbols for the sensual and/or for lust. Victorians did not discuss such subjects in polite society. Mouthing platitudes about the reverence of marriage, duty, and virtue, Victorian males often conducted extra-marital affairs with the blessings of a hypocritical society. Wilde expresses their repressed sexual drives with the hilarious scenes of his characters eating voraciously and discussing food. He also refers to sex and vitality with the euphemism of "health." When Algernon says that Gwendolen is "devoted to bread and butter," Jack immediately grabs some bread and butter and starts eating greedily.

Class warfare is also a subject of this first act. While the servants, such as Lane, wait on the upper classes, they also observe their morals.

They might not comment, but their facial expressions betray their understanding of their own role in life, which involves waiting and doing, but not commenting.

Style and manners also come under attack. In Victorian England, style and correct manners were much more important than substance. Algernon feels his style of piano playing is much more important than his accuracy. Triviality is the witty, admired social repartee of the day, a perfect homage to style over substance. In fact, the characters in this play often say the opposite of what is understood to be true. In this way Wilde shows his audience the hypocrisy of their commonly held beliefs.

Theme

Victorian culture is also a target. Algernon's quip, "More than half of modern culture depends on what one shouldn't read," is a reference once again to hypocrisy. Read something scandalous to be in style, but do not speak of it in polite company. Double standards abound. Daily newspapers come under Algernon's attack as the writings of people who have not been educated and who think of themselves as literary critics. Perhaps Wilde is saying that the critical reviews of the day should be in the hands of people who are educated to understand art.

Wilde's upper-class audiences, far from being angered by his attack on Victorian values, were actually mollified by references to locations and cultural names with which they were familiar. British names of real places such as Willis', Grosvenor Square, Tunbridge Wells in Kent, or Half Moon Street, would have been well-known references in their world. Upper-class London audiences recognized these familiar locations and knew the character types that Jack and Algernon represented.

Style & Language

Some critics have suggested that Wilde began his writing projects by accumulating a group of epigrams he wished to explore. (Often, these sayings about life were widely known but not really examined closely.) He turned these hackneyed phrases upside down to suggest that, although they knew the clichés, most British audiences did not stop to think about how meaningless they were. For example, "Divorces are made in heaven" (a corruption of the familiar "Marriages are made in heaven") suggests that divorce contributes to happiness—perhaps a greater truism than the familiar phrase given the tenor of Victorian society. Wilde makes fun of peoples' trivial concerns over social status when he says, "Nothing annoys people so much as not receiving invitations."

Style & Language

Wilde's use of language as a tool for humor continues with his hilarious puns. A *pun* is a wordplay that often involves differing understandings of what a word means and how it is used in a given context. In speaking of dentists and their *impressions,* Jack says, "It is very vulgar to talk like a dentist when one isn't a dentist. It produces a false impression." Algernon counters, "Well, that is exactly what dentists always do." False teeth, dental impressions to mold them, and social impressions are all wrapped up in this pun. In a society where turning a phrase and witty repartee were considered much-admired skills, Wilde was at his best.

Glossary

Half Moon Street   a very fashionable street in London's West End; its location is handy to gentlemen's clubs, restaurants, and theatres.

"slight refreshment at five o'clock"   known as light tea, served to people who visit at this time of day.

"Shropshire is your county"   a reference to Jack Worthing's position as county magistrate.

Divorce Court   Before 1857, divorces could only be granted by Parliament at great expense, and they rarely happened. In 1857, Divorce Court was passed by Parliament, making divorce easier.

Tunbridge Wells   a fashionable resort in Kent.

The Albany   Ernest Worthing's address on his calling cards was actually the home of George Ives, a friend of Wilde's and an activist for homosexual rights.

Bunbury   the name of a school friend of Wilde's. Here, someone who deceives.

sent down   to act as a lady's escort for dinner.

corrupt French Drama   possibly a reference to the plays of Alexander Dumas in the 1850s.

Act I—Part 2

Summary

Lady Bracknell and her daughter, Gwendolen, arrive. She is expecting her nephew, Algernon, at a dinner party that evening, but Algy explains that he must go see his invalid friend, Bunbury, in the country. However, he promises to make arrangements for the music at her reception on Saturday. They exchange small talk about various members of the upper class, and Lady Bracknell exclaims at the lack of cucumber sandwiches. The butler, Lane, lies beautifully, explaining there were no cucumbers in the market.

In an effort to leave Jack alone with Gwendolen, Algernon takes Lady Bracknell into another room to discuss music. Meanwhile, Jack proposes to Gwendolen; unfortunately, she explains that her ideal is to marry someone named Ernest and that Jack has no music or vibration to it. Nevertheless, she accepts his proposal, and Jack decides to arrange a private christening so that he can become Ernest. Lady Bracknell returns and, seeing Jack on bended knee, demands an explanation. Denying the engagement, she sends Gwendolen to the carriage.

Lady Bracknell interrogates Jack to determine his suitability. When Jack explains that he was found in a handbag abandoned in a railway station, Lady Bracknell is shocked. Jack goes on to explain that Mr. Thomas Cardew found him in Victoria Station and named him "Worthing" for the destination of his train ticket. Lady Bracknell announces that Gwendolen cannot "marry into a cloakroom, and form an alliance with a parcel." She advises Jack to find some relations. She bids him good morning and majestically sweeps out as Algernon plays the wedding march from the next room. Turning his thoughts to Cecily, Jack decides to kill off his "brother" Ernest with a severe chill in Paris because Cecily Cardew, his ward, is far too interested in the wicked Ernest, and as her guardian, Jack feels it his duty to protect her from inappropriate marriage suitors.

Gwendolen returns and tells Jack they can never marry, but she will always love him, and she will try to change her mother's mind. She asks for his country address so that she can write him daily and, as he dictates the address, Algernon furtively writes it on his own shirt cuff because he is curious about Cecily Cardew.

Commentary

Theme

The action and satire in Act I is heightened with the arrival of Lady Bracknell. She is an aristocratic Victorian and Algernon's aunt. Arrogant, opinionated, and conservative, Lady Bracknell is the epitome of the Victorian upper-class dowager. Wilde uses Lady Bracknell to continue his satire of Victorian attitudes about marriage. Marriage is a process of careful selection and planning by parents. Social status, lineage, and wealth combine to make marriage a business proposition that unites power. Lady Bracknell will tell Gwendolen when and to whom she will be engaged, and Gwendolen has nothing to say about it. In fact, love is not a factor in marriage nor is the opinion of the children. Lady Bracknell cross-examines Jack, commenting on his wealth and politics. When she hears Jack has "lost" his parents, she exclaims at his "carelessness." Discovering he is the accident of an unknown line of ancestors, she suggests he produce at least one parent—no matter how he does it—to strengthen his marriage prospects. Absurdly, Jack says he can produce the handbag, and it should satisfy her need for a parent. As for other examples of Wilde's opinions on marriage, Lady Bracknell mentions a recently widowed Lady Harbury who looks 20 years younger since her husband died, and now she lives for pleasure instead of duty. Wilde is mocking Victorian attitudes toward marriage and asking why bloodlines and wealth should be more important than love. Once again marriage is a duty, not a pleasure.

Theme

As for education, the proper Victorian believed schooling should continue the status quo, and "fortunately in England, at any rate, education produces no effect whatsoever. If it did, it would prove a serious danger to the upper classes, and probably lead to acts of violence in Grosvenor Square." A proper education is later echoed in the readings Miss Prism gives to Cecily Cardew, Jack's ward. Any revolution or change in thinking at any time is anathema to Lady Bracknell and the conservative upper class. Politics should be in the hands of the "right people." To the Victorian upper class, proper behavior, such as knowing who your parents are, keeps the standards where they should be. They feared that contempt for those things could lead to "the worst excesses of the French Revolution. And I presume you know what that unfortunate movement led to?" French aristocrats were executed, and Lady Bracknell would prefer to keep her head. Through the farcical Lady Bracknell, Wilde is once again criticizing a society where the upper class is determined to keep attitudes and power in the hands of the few; the radical idea that people should be taught to actually think and question is scary to those in power.

Theme

Wilde appears to be commenting on the traditional Victorian concept of family, also, where the restrictive bonds of duty smother initiative, imagination, and freedom. In Jack's case, Lady Bracknell feels family can be acquired, much like a luxurious home or expensive carriage. When Jack is critical of Lady Bracknell, instead of coming to his aunt's defense, Algernon says, "Relations are simply a tedious pack of people who haven't got the remotest knowledge of how to live, nor the smallest instinct about when to die." Both Jack and Algernon can escape to the country and change into different identities, escaping the duties of family. Jack would like to know his true identity, and Gwendolen would like to break away from her mother's conservative opinions. Wilde seems to foresee the phrase, *dysfunctional families.*

Character Insight

Gwendolen's middle name could be "absurdity." She trivializes serious ideas and imagines people and events that have never existed. Strangely, she chooses a husband based on his name. Wilde is asking if marrying for a person's name is any more intelligent, or absurd, than marrying based on wealth and parents. Wilde presents Gwendolen as a character who accepts the social order simply because it is defined from pulpits and popular magazines. Once again, Wilde is being critical of people who mouth the public sentiments and do not think for themselves. Gwendolen is also constantly saying words that are the opposite of what is known to be true, illustrating Wilde's idea that upper-class conversation is trivial and meaningless. She tells Jack, "the simplicity of your character makes you exquisitely incomprehensible to me." Instead of the young respecting their elders, Gwendolen laments, "Few parents nowadays pay any regard to what their children say to them. The old-fashioned respect for the young is fast dying out."

Literary Device

Jack's proposal itself is ludicrous. Gwendolen is only concerned that the form is correct. In fact, she fully intends to say yes only if his name is Ernest. When Jack mentions the word marriage, she protests that he has not even discussed it with her yet, and he must do so in the correct style. She asserts that her brother even practices proposing to get the form correct. Wilde is taking a subject—love and marriage—that should be filled with passion and depth and turning it into an exercise in form. This scene is a parody of love and romance, capturing the emptiness of Victorian values that rely on style, not substance.

Theme

Throughout Act I, Wilde's characters worship the trivial at the expense of the profound. He seems to be saying that the audience should take a long look at what their society deems valuable. Society is described in multiple contexts as clever people talking nonsense and triviality. In a dialogue between Jack and Algernon, Jack says, "I am sick to death of cleverness. Everybody is clever nowadays. You can't go anywhere without meeting clever people. The thing has become an absolute public nuisance. I wish to goodness we had a few fools left." When Algernon says, "We have," Jack wonders what they talk about. Algernon replies, "about the clever people, of course." Wilde continues satirizing the Victorian love of the trivial when he ends the act with Jack and Algernon observing that nobody ever talks anything but nonsense. Each of these conversations reprimands British society's concern for the superficial at the expense of deeper values.

What subjects should a society take seriously? Wilde obviously thought society should revere sympathy and compassion for others. But Lady Bracknell treats the very human concerns of death and illness with irreverence and flippancy. She tells Algernon, "It is high time that Mr. Bunbury made up his mind whether he was going to live or to die. This shilly-shallying with the question is absurd." Furthermore, she does not think a person's illnesses should be encouraged. Rather than being sympathetic, she hopes Mr. Bunbury will not have a relapse on Saturday, thus throwing a wrench in her party plans. Again, by having the farcical Lady Bracknell express these thoughts, Wilde conveys his desire for his audience to question their tendency to value social calendars at the expense of sympathy for others.

Character Insight

The subject of Cecily introduces a new kind of woman to the play. When Algy expresses some interest in Jack's ward, Jack explains that she is not at all like the usual young woman in society. "She has got a capital appetite, goes on long walks, and pays no attention at all to her lessons." Unlike most young Victorian women, Cecily is independent, strong, and can figure out what she wants. Her description intrigues Algy, and plans start simmering in his head.

Character Insight

Besides using the character of Algernon to comment on the values of Victorian society, Wilde also uses him to illuminate the lifestyle of the young dandy or aesthete. When Jack and Algernon discuss their evening plans, it is described as hard work: "Shall we go out for dinner? Go to the theatre? Go to the club? Go to the Empire?" When Algy asks what they should do, Jack says, "Nothing!" Algernon retorts, "It is awfully hard work doing nothing." To take little seriously, to not work, and to artfully cultivate the air of doing nothing were all poses of the aesthetes. Algernon also tears up bills that arrive, illustrating the casual attitude of dandies toward responsibilities.

Style & Language

As the play progresses, Wilde continues his epigrams and puns. One of his most memorable refers to the nature of men and women. Algernon explains, "All women become like their mothers. That is their tragedy. No man does. That's his." Perhaps Wilde feels that while women might not wish to become their mothers, men would be wise to cultivate some of the attitudes and values of females; perhaps this is a nod to homosexuality. Throughout the act, epigrams deliver Wilde's social commentary on families, men and women, marriage, status, and the values of the upper class. A common lament of the titled gentry is also satirically mentioned by Lady Bracknell when discussing Jack's wealth: "What between the duties expected of one during one's lifetime, and the duties exacted from one after one's death, land has ceased to be either a profit or a pleasure. It gives one position, and prevents one from keeping it up." The use of the word *duties* is a delicious pun also. It means both the duties a person is expected to do according to his position and taxes placed on estates by the government.

Glossary

Grosvenor Square   a very affluent area of London in the Mayfair district.

Belgrave Square   another affluent London area in Belgravia.

Liberal Unionist   a political group that voted against Home Rule for Ireland in 1886. Liberals were the conservative political group.

Tories   members of the more conservative political circles. Lady Bracknell and other wealthy socialites would approve.

"only eighteen"   Cecily is the precise age to "come out" as a Society debutante. During the Season, 18-year-olds were introduced as marriage material for suitable men.

The Empire   a theatre in Leicester Square, London.

The Railway Guide   an indispensable timetable of railway departures and arrivals, probably invented by Robert Diggles Kay in either 1838 or 1839.

Act II—Part 1

Summary

Act II is set at Jack Worthing's country estate where Miss Prism is seated in the garden giving her student, Cecily Cardew, a lesson in German grammar. When Cecily expresses an interest in meeting Jack's wicked brother, Ernest, Miss Prism repeats Jack's opinion that his brother has a weak character. The governess knows what happens to people who have weak characters. In her younger days, Miss Prism wrote a three-volume novel, and she proclaims that fiction shows how good people end happily and bad people end unhappily.

The local reverend, Canon Chasuble, enters and flirts with Miss Prism. The two leave for a turn in the garden. While they are gone, Merriman, the butler, announces Mr. Ernest Worthing has just arrived with his luggage and is anxious to speak with Miss Cardew. Algernon comes in, pretending to be Jack's brother, Ernest. When Cecily says that Jack is coming to the country Monday afternoon, Algernon/Ernest announces that he will be leaving Monday morning. They will just miss each other. Algernon compliments her beauty, and they go inside just before Miss Prism and Dr. Chasuble return.

Jack enters in mourning clothes because his brother Ernest is dead in Paris. Jack takes the opportunity to ask Dr. Chasuble to re-christen him that afternoon around 5 p.m. Cecily comes from the house and announces that Jack's brother Ernest is in the dining room. Oops. Ernest is supposed to be dead. Algernon comes out, and Jack is shocked. Algernon/Ernest vows to reform and lead a better life.

Jack is angry that Algernon could play such a trick. He orders the dogcart for Algernon to leave in. After Jack goes into the house, Algernon announces he is in love with Cecily. Algernon proclaims his undying affection while Cecily copies his words in her diary. Algernon asks Cecily to marry him, and she agrees. In fact, she agrees readily because she has made up an entire romantic story of their courtship and engagement. She has even written imaginary letters to herself from Ernest/Algernon. She tells Algernon that her dream has always been to marry someone named Ernest because the name inspires such confidence. So, like Jack, Algernon decides he must be re-christened Ernest.

Commentary

Act II expands on many of the motifs introduced in Act I, but adds new characters and targets for Wilde's satire. The setting changes to the country—a bucolic setting for getting away from the artificial trappings of society and entering the simplicity of nature—and Wilde examines religion as well as courtship and marriage in the context of Victorian attitudes. But even in the countryside, the characters cannot escape Victorian manners and correctness, as the name Ernest presents humorous complications.

Theme

Idleness, duty, and marriage are brought together in the conversations of several characters. Sighing bitterly, Miss Prism observes that people who live for pleasure are usually unmarried. Duty, duty, duty. Servant of the upper class, Prism sees responsibility tinted with obligation as the correct form in Victorian society. Cecily, however, exclaims to Miss Prism, "I suppose that is why he [Jack] often looks a little bored when we three are together." In subtitling his play *A Trivial Comedy for Serious People,* perhaps Wilde is showing that setting one's jaw in a strong position for living rigidly with duty is both shortsighted and tediously boring.

Miss Prism and Canon Chasuble also provide a comic touch to the subject of religious zeal and its relationship to Victorian morals. Religion is presented as dry, meaningless, and expensive. The minister explains to Jack that the sermons for all sacraments are interchangeable. They can be adapted to be joyful or distressing, depending on the occasion. Through these thoughts Wilde expresses the meaninglessness of religion and the obviously hackneyed, empty words of sermons. Jack's request for a christening is humorous when one considers that he is a grown man—christening is a rite usually appropriate for small babies.

Wilde humorously captures the absurdity of rigid Victorian values when he utilizes Miss Prism as his mouthpiece, a morally upright woman who has, nevertheless, written a melodramatic, romantic novel. Obviously, hypocrisy lurks beneath the strict, puritanical surface of the prim governess. The height of her absurdity over rigid morals comes when she hears that Ernest is dead in Paris after a life of "shameful debts and extravagance." As if to follow through on her duty to raise Cecily with rigid values, she says, "What a lesson for him! I trust he will profit by it."

Literary Device

The Victorian mania to exclude anyone and everyone who did not conform to social norms is touched on by Wilde's satire of reform movements. His words come from Miss Prism when she says, "I am not in favour of this modern mania for turning bad people into good people at a moment's notice." Wilde is referring here to the duty of the upper class to provide moral role models and convert those who are wicked to the "good" way of life. An endless number of societies existed for the reform of various causes. Algy gleefully utilizes the ruse of helplessness when he begs Cecily to reform him. However, she explains, "I'm afraid I've no time, this afternoon." Reform must have occurred quickly in 1890s' England. One of the clearest expressions of Wilde satirizing his upper-class audience members is in the words of the minister. Chasuble is discussing his sermons and mentions that he gave a charity sermon on behalf of the Society for the Prevention of Discontent Among the Upper Orders. This name is a parody of the long names of various societies that the wealthy dallied with in their quest for redemption.

The hidden and repressed sexual nature of Victorian society is emphasized in Act II. Cecily is fascinated by sin and wickedness—but from afar. She hopes Ernest looks like a "wicked person," although she is not sure what one looks like. She is particularly interested in the fact that the prim and proper Miss Prism has written a three-volume novel. Such novels were not deemed proper literature by Victorians, but were read in secret. Of course, the moral of the novel shows clearly that good people win, and bad people are punished. In fact, Miss Prism describes the conservative literary view of the day when she defines fiction as "the good ended happily, and the bad unhappily." As always, these rewards or punishments occur in a clear-cut manner and without exception—in novels.

Character Insight

Much worldlier than Cecily, the canon and Miss Prism flirt outrageously and make innuendoes about desire and lust. Where a headache is usually used as an excuse for a lack of sexual interest, Miss Prism uses it as a reason to go on a walk alone with the minister. The humorous cleric speaks in metaphors and often has to define what he means so that he will not be misunderstood. For example, he states, "Were I fortunate enough to be Miss Prism's pupil, I would hang upon her lips." His words elicit a glare from the prim Miss Prism. He continues to put his foot in his mouth by saying, "I spoke metaphorically. My metaphor was drawn from bees. Ahem!" Such an obvious allusion to the birds and the bees thinly veils a passionate inner life that must not be discussed. Miss Prism answers in kind, calling him "dear Doctor," which seems to be a flirtatious title. There is more than meets the eye here, and Wilde is clearly pointing out the sexual repression of his society and satirizing the societal concern for correct and proper appearances, regardless of what simmers under the surface.

The coded conversation between Miss Prism and Chasuble eventually turns to the discussion of the canon's celibacy, which becomes a joke throughout the act. When he defends the church's stand on celibacy, Miss Prism explains that remaining single is actually more of a temptation to women. To a Victorian audience, *maturity, ripeness,* and *green* are all coded words dealing with experience and naiveté. Suddenly, the canon realizes he has been saying things that might be interpreted as improper; he hastily covers up with, "I spoke horticulturally. My metaphor was drawn from fruits." All his veiled remarks reflect the cryptic nature of sexual experiences in the world of the 1890s. It is a world where adults do not discuss sex directly with their children or in polite society. No wonder Cecily is so fascinated by the subject of wickedness. In her society, young girls are protected from any knowledge of sex, and adults speak of it in obscure terms so as not to let out the big secret.

Class boundaries are also represented by the minister and Miss Prism. As the local canon, Chasuble is at Jack's beck and call and takes his orders from Jack and the local magistrate. If anyone needs a particular ceremony or sermon, the minister is ready to assist. While he is a scholarly man, Chasuble is still at the bottom of the social ladder in the countryside. Miss Prism must earn her living as a governess, and she too is a servant of the wealthy.

Theme

Cecily's schooling is a perfect opportunity for Wilde to comment on the grim, unimaginative education of England. Cecily is over protected lest her imagination run wild. Plain, guttural German is lauded, and Cecily feels plain after reciting it. "The Fall of the Rupee" is seen as "too sensational" for her to read. Political economy was a fast growing academic subject at the time—the province of male students, not young women. Grim, conservative, and unimaginative books are seen as the best way to educate the young. With this foundation, they learn not to question and not to change dramatically the society in which they live. Promoting the status quo is the goal of such learning—an idea that was an anathema to Wilde, hence his desire to satirize it.

Literary Device

Merriman's humor is a foil—or opposite—for Jack's seriousness. Even his name indicates his hidden humor. During the argument about Algernon taking a dogcart back to London, Merriman good-humoredly goes along with Cecily and Jack in the tugging to and fro of Algernon. While he does not express approval or disapproval, he accommodates his upper-class employers and carefully rehearses his facial expressions to show nothing, but through this deliberate rehearsal, Wilde is showing what an artificial, rehearsed society the upper class inhabits. Merriman's job is to orchestrate comings and goings and keep the house running smoothly; he's a proper English servant who knows his place. Similarly, Miss Prism chastises Cecily for watering flowers—a servant's job. By presenting these vignettes—subtle, carefully constructed literary sketches—within the context of a farce, Wilde pokes fun at the Victorian concept that everyone has his duty, and each knows his place.

In Act II, Wilde also exposes the vacuity of the Victorian obsession with appearance. Algernon declares to Cecily that he would never let Jack pick his clothing because, "He has no taste in neckties at all." Clothing is appearance, and appearance is everything. When Algernon travels to the country for just a few short days, he brings "three portmanteaus, a dressing-case, two hat boxes, and a large luncheon-basket." Once again, trifling subjects command excessive attention.

Character Insight

Cecily keeps a diary of her girlish fancies, and they are much more interesting than reality. Because her education is so dry and boring, she lives an interesting fantasy life, which comprises her own secret and self-directed education. She, like Algernon, seems to be interested in immediate gratification, and she puts him in his place when she first meets him. When he calls her "little cousin Cecily," she counters with, "You are under some strange mistake. I am not little. In fact, I believe I am more than usually tall for my age." Algernon is totally taken aback by her forwardness. Wilde here is hinting at a new and more assertive woman.

Theme

Wilde also begins an attack on the concepts of romance and courtship in Act II. Gwendolen and Jack have already demonstrated that proposals must be made correctly, especially if anyone is nearby. Now, Cecily and Algernon present a mockery of conventional courtship and romance. As always, appearance is everything. Cecily's diary is a particularly useful tool to symbolize the deceptive character of romance and courtship. When Miss Prism tells Cecily that memory is all one needs to remember one's life, Cecily replies, "Yes, but it usually chronicles the things that have never happened, and couldn't possibly have happened." False memory is what provides for the romance in Miss Prism's three-volume novel. Young girls' heads are filled with romance and naïve ideas about marriage; the true nature of courtship in Victorian, upper-class society is a business deal, according to Wilde, where financial security and family names are traded for wives. Wilde shows this clearly when Algernon proposes to Cecily and tells her he loves her. He is a bit confused when she explains that they have already been engaged for three months, starting last February 14—at least that is how she recorded her fantasy in her diary. In fact, she even mentions where, when, and how their engagement took place. Furthermore, she has letters written by Ernest that purport his love and chronicle the breaking off of the engagement. (No engagement is serious if it is not broken off at least once and then forgiven.) Comically, she mentions in passing that Ernest has beautiful words but that they are "badly spelled." Through this comment, Wilde highlights the superficial Victorian approach to courtship and marriage by having Cecily criticize the spelling in a love letter. To emphasize this absurdity, Algernon comments on the weather in the same breath as their engagement.

Glossary

"As a man sows, so let him reap."   This is a verse from the *Bible*, Galatians 6:7, meaning that actions determine fate.

three-volume novels   Lending libraries circulated novels in three parts so that three different readers could be reading at the same time. This practice ended in the late 1800s.

Mudie   a lending library.

egeria   chastity. Egeri, a nymph, gave wise laws to Numa Pompilius of Rome that were used for the vestal virgins.

Evensong   a Sunday evening religious service.

womanthrope   a humorous word made up by Miss Prism for a person who hates women.

sententiously   full of, or fond of using, maxims, proverbs and so on, especially in a way that is ponderously trite and moralizing.

the Primitive Church   the pre-Reformation Catholic Church, whose priest remained celibate.

canonical practice   church law.

Act II—Part 2
Summary

While Algernon rushes out to make christening arrangements, Cecily writes Ernest's proposal in her diary. She is interrupted by Merriman announcing The Honorable Gwendolen Fairfax to see Jack; unfortunately, Jack is at the rectory. Cecily asks her in, and they introduce themselves. Gwendolen did not know Jack had a ward, and she wishes Cecily were older and less beautiful.

Both announce that they are engaged to Ernest Worthing. When they compare diaries, they decide that Gwendolen was asked first; however, Cecily says that since then, he has obviously changed his mind and proposed to Cecily. Merriman and a footman enter with tea, which stops their argument. They discuss geography and flowers in a civilized manner while the servants are present. However, during the tea ceremony, Cecily deliberately gives Gwendolen sugar in her tea when Gwendolen did not want sugar and tea cake when Gwendolen expressly asked for bread and butter. The situation is very tense and strained.

Jack arrives, and Gwendolen calls him Ernest; he kisses Gwendolen who demands an explanation of the situation. Cecily explains that this is not Ernest but her guardian, Jack Worthing. Algernon comes in, and Cecily calls him Ernest. Gwendolen explains that he is her cousin, Algernon Moncrieff. The ladies then console each other because the men have played a monstrous trick on them. Jack sheepishly admits that he has no brother Ernest and has never had a brother of any kind. Both ladies announce that they are not engaged to anyone and leave to go into the house.

Commentary

Act II explores the personalities of Cecily Cardew and Gwendolen Fairfax. Both women have in common their singled-minded persistence in pursuing a husband named Ernest. They have strong opinions, are able to deal with unexpected situations, and are connected in many instances by dialogue that is repetitive and parallel. However, they also have many differences.

Cecily Cardew is passionate about her desires and her goals, but she is also overly protected in the country setting. She is being brought up far away from the temptations and social life of the city, protected until her coming out. Her goal is to marry a solid Victorian husband with the trustworthy name of Ernest. When she meets Algernon, she is sure she has found him.

Gwendolen Fairfax is a big-city, sophisticated woman in sharp contrast to Cecily Cardew. Gwendolen has ideas of her own. Like her mother, Gwendolen is determined. Gwendolen knows what she wants. She comes to the country to pursue her Ernest, thinking she will rescue him. She tells Cecily, "If the poor fellow has been entrapped into any foolish promise, I shall consider it my duty to rescue him at once, and with a firm hand." Whatever her opinion, she states it very clearly. With her lorgnette, she views her world with the shortsightedness instilled in her by her Victorian mother—like mother, like daughter. However, this daughter occasionally chafes at the restraints placed on her by her class and time period. Humorously, Wilde displays Gwendolen's shortsightedness when he mentions her diary. Gwendolen's thoughts generally consist of observations about herself. She is totally self-absorbed, like most of the characters in Wilde's play.

Wilde links Cecily and Gwendolen very cleverly by using parallel conversations and by repeating bits and pieces of sentences. They both discuss liking and disliking each other with exactly the same words. Likewise, they both discuss marrying Ernest with the same phrases. Gwendolen says, "My first impressions of people are never wrong," and later counters with, "My first impressions of people are invariably right." Their artificial speech and comments on trivial subjects are part of polite conversation. Jack and Algernon are also linked with parallel lines that display the similarities in their situations. Jack says, "You won't be able to run down to the country quite so often as you used to do, dear Algy. And a very good thing too." Algernon parallels this line with "You won't be able to disappear to London quite so frequently as your wicked custom was. And not a bad thing either." The parallel words and lines are used almost like a minuet, where each partner circles around the other turning one way and then the other. Wilde has choreographed the lines to present a stylized, artificial milieu that exaggerates the art of manners and social discourse.

The culmination of Wilde's commentary on Victorian social rituals is the tea ceremony with Cecily and Gwendolen. This witty exchange of conversation is representative of Victorian social ritual where proposals, social calls, and parties are all carefully orchestrated. Because it is conducted under obvious duress, the tea becomes a ridiculous event. Throughout the tea pouring and the cake cutting, Cecily and Gwendolen are mindful of their manners in front of the servants. Even their anger is civilized. Once the servants leave they discover they are engaged to the same man, and the conversation heats up considerably. The servants, however, provide a calming influence, and the women must simply glare at each other across the table. Their sarcasm is revealed in Wilde's stage directions. When Cecily makes a satirical comment about Gwendolen living in town because she does not like crowds—indicating that she has few friends and little social life—Gwendolen bites her lip and beats her foot nervously. Cecily is instructed to make this comment "sweetly." For her own part, Gwendolen calls Cecily a detestable girl, but her comment is made in an aside to the audience.

Literary Device

For their part, the servants continue to serve as an opportunity for Wilde to comment on the all-knowing-but-seldom-commenting lower class. Merriman's function is to announce people and events, warn of the approach of Lady Bracknell with a discrete cough, and watch the happenings with amusement but without registering this with his face or manners. He carries to the tea ceremony all the traditional hardware: a salver, a tablecloth, and a plate stand. Wilde says in his directions, "The presence of the servants exercises a restraining influence . . ." The women know they must not bicker in front of the hired help, and the servants understand that their very proximity will play a role in the outcome. Merriman asserts his mistress's role when he asks Cecily if he should lay the tea "as usual." Cecily answers, "sternly, in a calm voice, 'Yes, as usual.'" Mistress and servant are acknowledging her role as the lady of the house. Wilde seems to be asking what the British upper class would do without the stern but calming influence of its servants.

Several motifs that have been mentioned earlier are continued in this scene. Religion is once again referred to as a matter of form and format. The significance of a person's baptism is not even a matter for concern when Jack and Algernon get the canon to agree to baptize them. A person's rebirth is only a matter of a name on a piece of paper. It is a means to an end because it will get both men what they want: Cecily and Gwendolen.

Reform comes to mean the possibility that dissenters can be taught to see the error of their ways and conform to the status quo. Cecily's education is grooming her to be a member of the upper class, mindlessly repeating its virtues. She offers to reform Algernon, acting with forward zeal. She plans to turn Algernon into the perfect Ernest, a man who will be like other men and propose correctly, protect and support her financially, and stop his single life on the town.

Conventional Victorian values and behavior are often the subjects of bantering among the characters in this scene. Gwendolen is pleased that "outside the family circle" her father is unknown. Certainly idle gossip about the wealthy should not be a matter of public discussion. The appearance of Victorian family life is for the man to be part of the domestic setting, but, as always, Wilde is saying that this appearance is the ideal while the reality is quite different.

Truth and deception also continue to be a part of Wilde's country world. Gwendolen passionately comments on Jack's honest and upright nature. "He is the very soul of truth and honour. Disloyalty would be as impossible to him as deception." Of course, the audience knows that her Ernest has lied about himself throughout the course of their courtship. Algernon also engages in deception in this scene when he acknowledges that his trip to Jack's estate has been the most wonderful bunburying trip of his life. What began as trivial has become an engagement. Both men accuse each other of deceiving the women in their lives, and Jack says that Algernon cannot marry Cecily because he has been deceptive to her. Alternatively, Algernon accuses Jack of engaging in deception toward his cousin, Gwendolen. By the end of the scene, it seems that marriage plans will not materialize for either of them anytime soon. Their deception as Ernests is definitely over, and now they must figure out how to pick up the pieces. The hypocrisy of Victorian virtues, paid lip service in public but invariably denied in private lives, is aptly represented by Jack and Algernon's behavior.

Glossary

effeminate   having the qualities generally attributed to women, such as weakness, timidity, delicacy, and so on; unmanly; not virile.

the Morning Post   a newspaper read by the upper class because of its reporting on engagements, marriages, and social gossip.

lorgnette   a pair of eyeglasses attached to a handle.

"a restraining influence"   the presence of servants that causes the principal characters to be careful in their speech.

machinations   an artful or secret plot or scheme.

Act III

Summary

No time has elapsed, but in Act III Gwendolen and Cecily are in the morning room of the Manor House, looking out the window at Jack and Algernon and hoping they will come in. If they do, the ladies intend to be cold and heartless. The men do come in and start explaining why they lied about their names. The women accept their explanations but still have a problem with them lacking the name Ernest. Both men proclaim that they plan to be rechristened, and Gwendolen and Cecily forgive them, and both couples embrace.

Merriman discretely coughs to signal the entrance of Lady Bracknell. She desires an explanation for these hugs, and Gwendolen tells her that she is engaged to Jack. Lady Bracknell says that they are not engaged and insists that they cease all communication. She inquires about Algernon's invalid friend, Bunbury, and Algernon explains that he killed him that afternoon; Bunbury exploded. He also adds that he and Cecily are engaged. Immediately, Lady Bracknell interrogates Jack about Cecily's expectations. However, because she has a fortune of 130,000 pounds, Lady Bracknell believes her to have "distinct social possibilities."

Lady Bracknell gives her consent to Algernon's engagement, but Jack immediately objects as Cecily's guardian. He says that Algernon is a liar and lists all the lies he has told. Also, Cecily does not come into her fortune and lose Jack as a guardian until she is 35 years old. Algernon says he can wait, but Cecily says she cannot. So Jack, in a moment of brilliance, declares that he will agree to the marriage if Lady Bracknell will consent to his engagement to Gwendolen. That is out of the question, and Lady Bracknell prepares to leave with Gwendolen.

Dr. Chasuble arrives and announces that he is ready for the christenings. Jack replies that they are useless now, and Chasuble decides to head back to the church where Miss Prism is waiting. The name Prism shocks Lady Bracknell, and she demands to see the governess. When Miss Prism arrives, she sees Lady Bracknell and turns pale. In a moment of great coincidence, Lady Bracknell reveals that Miss Prism left Lord Bracknell's house 28 years ago. On a normal walk with the baby carriage, she disappeared, along with the baby. She demands to know where the baby is. Prism explains that in a moment of great distraction, she placed the baby in her handbag and her three-volume, manuscript in the baby carriage. The baby and handbag were accidentally left in the train station. When she discovered her error, she abandoned the baby carriage and disappeared. Jack excitedly asks her which station it was, and when she reveals that it was Victoria Station, the Brighton Line, he runs from the room and returns with a black leather bag. When Prism identifies it, he embraces her, believing her to be his mother. She protests that she is not married and says that he will have to ask Lady Bracknell for the identity of his mother.

Jack discovers that he is actually the son of Lady Bracknell's sister, Mrs. Moncrieff, and that Algy is his older brother. Jack is overcome to know that he really does have an unfortunate scoundrel for a brother. He asks what his christened name was, and Lady Bracknell explains that it is Ernest John. So, Jack asserts that he had been speaking the truth all along: His name is Ernest, and he does have a brother. Both couples embrace, as do Chasuble and Miss Prism, and Jack declares that he finally realizes the importance of being earnest.

Commentary

Act III offers happy resolution to the problems of identity and marriage that drive much of the humor in the previous acts. Wilde continues to mock the social customs and attitudes of the aristocratic class. He relentlessly attacks their values, views on marriage and respectability, sexual attitudes, and concern for stability in the social structure.

Theme

Wilde attacks social behavior with the continuation of speeches by his characters that are the opposite of their actions. While Cecily and Gwendolen agree to keep a dignified silence, Gwendolen actually states that they will not be the first ones to speak to the men. In the very next line she says, "Mr. Worthing, I have something very particular to ask you." Wilde seems to be saying that people speak as if they have strong opinions, but their actions do not support their words. If actions truly do speak louder than words, Wilde has made his point: Society, literally, speaks volumes, but the words are meaningless.

Wilde continues his criticism of society's valuing style over substance when Gwendolen says, "In matters of grave importance, style, not sincerity is the vital thing." Lady Bracknell discusses Algernon's marriage assets in the same light. She says, "Algernon is an extremely, I may almost say an ostentatiously, eligible young man. He has nothing, but he looks everything. What more can one desire?" Indeed, in a society where looks are everything and substance is discounted, Algernon is the perfect husband.

Theme

What else do aristocrats value? They seem to esteem the appearance of respectability. Respectability means children are born within the context of marriage. Wilde once again mocks the hypocrisy of the aristocrats who appear to value monogamy but pretend not to notice affairs. Jack's speech to Miss Prism, whom he believes to be his mother, is humorous in both its indignant defense of marriage and also its mocking of the loudly touted religious reformer's virtues of repentance and forgiveness. He says to Miss Prism, "Unmarried! I do not deny that is a serious blow . . . Mother, I forgive you." His words are all the more humorous when Miss Prism indignantly denies being his mother. It was not at all unusual for aristocrats to have children born out of wedlock, but society turned its head, pretended not to know about those children, and did not condemn their fathers.

The gulf between the upper class and its servants is explored in the scenes with Merriman and Prism. When Lady Bracknell unexpectedly shows up at Jack's, Merriman coughs discretely to warn the couples of her arrival. One can only imagine his humorous thoughts as he watches the wealthy tiptoe around each other and argue about what should be important. When Lady Bracknell hears the description of Prism and recognizes her as their former nanny, she calls for Miss Prism by shouting "Prism!" without using a title in front of her name. Imperiously, Lady Bracknell divides the servant from the lady of the manor. Wilde's audience would recognize this behavior on the part of the servants and the upper class. The stuffy class distinctions defined the society in which they lived.

In an age of social registers, Lady Bracknell laments that even the Court Guides have errors. In the next breath, she discusses bribing Gwendolen's maid to find out what is happening in her daughter's life. In Act III she also reveals that her aristocratic brother's family entrusted their most precious possession—Jack—to a woman who is more interested in her handbag and manuscript than in what happens to the baby in her charge. Wilde seems to be questioning the values of a society that believes in social registers, hires other people to neglectfully watch its children, and uses bribery to keep track of the children who are not missing.

The death of Bunbury gives Wilde the opportunity to speak of aristocratic fears and have some continued fun with the upper class's lack of compassion about death. The 1885 Trafalgar Square riots brought on ruling-class fears of insurrection, anarchism, and socialism. Wilde humorously touches on these fears when he allows Algernon to explain the explosion of Bunbury. Lady Bracknell, fearing the worst, exclaims,

"Was he the victim of a revolutionary outrage? I was not aware that Mr. Bunbury was interested in social legislation. If so, he is well punished for his morbidity." Evidently, to Lady Bracknell's acquaintances, laws that protect the welfare of those less fortunate are strictly morbid subjects. In fact, this attitude seems to contradict the upper-class concern for reform. However, in reality, Wilde is confirming the upper-class definition of social reform: conforming to the status quo.

Style & Language

In Act III Wilde makes a comment on the value of being homosexual with a veiled reference to Lady Lancing. When Lady Bracknell asserts that Cecily needs to have a more sophisticated hairstyle, she recommends "a thoroughly experienced French maid" who can make a great deal of change in a very short time. She explains that such a change happened to an acquaintance of hers, Lady Lancing, and that after three months "her own husband did not know her." Jack uses the opportunity to make a pun on the word *know,* using it in an aside— a comment only the audience can hear. Jack interprets *know* to mean they no longer had sex, insinuating Lady Lancing's preference for the French maid. He says, "And after six months nobody knew her," indicating that the homosexual experience made a new woman of her. Although homosexuality would have been seen as immoral to Wilde's audience, Jack indicates that being homosexual might be a good thing—almost as a social commentary—directly to the audience. It seems a double life is necessary after one is married, whether it be bunburying or the homosexual life Wilde was experiencing in an increasingly public way.

Theme

Wilde continues his assault on family life in Act III by mentioning its strange qualities in several conversations. It appears rather strange, for example, that Lady Bracknell cannot even recall the Christian name of her brother-in-law, Algy's father. Algernon's father died before Algernon was one, so stranger yet is Algernon's comment, "We were never even on speaking terms." He gives that as the reason he cannot remember his father's name. Further assaulting family life, Wilde has Lady Bracknell describe Lord Moncrieff as "eccentric" but excuses his behavior because it "was the result of the Indian climate, and marriage, and indigestions, and other things of that kind." Marriage is lumped together with things such as indigestion. In explaining Lord Moncrieff's marriage, Lady Bracknell says that he was "essentially a man of peace, except in his domestic life." Her description invites suspicion that the local constabulary might have visited because of domestic disturbances. Family life and domestic bliss do not get high marks in Wilde's estimation.

When Miss Prism humorously resolves the problem of Jack's lineage, Wilde takes his hero of unknown origins and paints him as the aristocrat who will now be assimilated into his rightful place in the social structure. Through the sad melodrama of Jack's handbag parentage, Wilde exaggerates the Victorian cliché of the poor foundling who makes good. As soon as Jack is known to be a member of the established aristocracy, a Moncrieff in fact, he is seen as an appropriate person for Gwendolen to marry. They will, according to Wilde, live happily ever after in wedded bliss and continue the aristocratic blindness to anything that truly matters.

Character Insight

The tag line of the play, spoken by Jack, is a familiar convention in Victorian farces. In discovering that he has been telling the truth all along—his name is Ernest, and he has a brother—Jack makes fun of the Victorian virtues of sincerity and honesty and asks Gwendolen to forgive him for "speaking nothing but the truth." He now realizes the importance of being the person he is supposed to be. Wilde is saying perhaps that a new kind of earnestness exists, one that is different from the virtues extolled by the Victorians. Maybe it is possible to be honest and understand what should be taken seriously in life rather than being deceptive, hypocritical, and superficial. Some readers believe, however, that the ending shows Jack mockingly redefining Victorian earnestness as just the opposite: a life of lies, pleasure, and beauty. Critics debate the interpretation of the last line.

Style & Language

A curious stage direction occurs in Act III, revealing the concern Wilde had for the staging of his play to compliment his ideas. As his couples come together and move apart, he emphasizes the choreography of the pairs. He has them speak in unison, both the women together and the men together. It matters not who they are; they are interchangeable. Marriage is simply an institution that is a gesture, like a christening. The unison speaking is very stylistic, not meant to be realistic at all. It reveals Wilde's attitude that what is important in Victorian marriage—names—really should not be as important as other considerations.

In the end, Wilde leaves his audience thinking about the trivial social conventions they deem important. Their Victorian virtues perhaps need redefining. Institutions such as marriage, religion, family values and money should perhaps have new interpretations. The character of people, rather than their names and family fortunes, should weigh most heavily when considering their worth. Wilde was able to use humor to skewer these attitudes and convince his audience about the importance of being earnest.

Glossary

effrontery unashamed boldness.

German skepticism a German philosophy that examines style or appearance rather than substance.

University Extension Scheme The University of London began these extension courses that were early developments in adult education.

terminus (British) either the end of a transportation line, or a station or town located there; terminal.

Court Guides an annual reference manual listing the names and addresses of members of the upper class and aristocracy.

Funds government stocks that give a low yield of interest but are conservative and safe.

Oxonian someone who graduated from Oxford University.

Anabaptists a religious group that believes the only form of baptism should be complete immersion of the body in water.

pew-opener a person who works for a church by opening the private pews of the wealthy.

perambulator (chiefly British) a baby carriage; buggy.

Temperance beverage a drink that expressly does not contain alcohol.

Army Lists published lists of commissioned officers in the British Army.

CHARACTER ANALYSES

The following critical analyses delve into the physical, emotional, and psychological traits of the literary work's major characters so that you might better understand what motivates these characters. The writer of this study guide provides this scholarship as an educational tool by which you may compare your own interpretations of the characters. Before reading the character analyses that follow, consider first writing your own short essays on the characters as an exercise by which you can test your understanding of the original literary work. Then, compare your essays to those that follow, noting discrepancies between the two. If your essays appear lacking, that might indicate that you need to re-read the original literary work or re-familiarize yourself with the major characters.

John (Jack) Worthing

Jack Worthing, like the other main characters in Wilde's play, is less a realistic character and more an instrument for representing a set of ideas or attitudes. Wilde uses him to represent an upper-class character easily recognized by his audience. Jack also gives Wilde an opportunity to explore attitudes about Victorian rituals such as courtship and marriage. As an alter ego of Wilde, Jack represents the idea of leading a life of respectability on the surface (in the country) and a life of deception for pleasure (in the city). His name, Worthing, is related to worthiness, allowing Wilde to humorously consider the correct manners of Victorian society.

As a recognized upper-class Victorian, Jack has earned respectability only because of his adopted father's fortune. It has put him in a position to know the rules of behavior of polite society. His ability to spout witty lines about trivial subjects and say the opposite of what is known to be true are learned results of his position. When Lady Bracknell questions his qualifications for marrying her daughter, he knows she wants to hear about his pedigree. He recognizes that he needs the correct parents along with his wealth.

Of particular significance is Jack's role in the dialogues about social attitudes and rituals, such as courtship and marriage. He often plays the straight man to counter Algernon's humor, but occasionally, he gets the witty lines. Respectability is also a function of Jack's character. Although he leads a deceptive life in town, he represents the ideal of leading a responsible life in the country. He agrees more with the idea of Victorian earnestness or duty than Algernon does. However, because he deceives people in the city, he is still a symbol of Wilde's deceptive life of pleasure in the homosexual community. Jack longs for the respectability of marrying Gwendolen and is willing to do whatever it takes. In the long run, he assumes his rightful place in the very society he has occasionally skewered for its attitudes. Wilde is able to soften Jack's respectability and position as a symbol of the ruling class by showing his enormous sense of humor. The funeral garb for his fake brother's death and the story about the French maid both show that while Jack longs for respectability, he still has the wit and rebelliousness to recognize the ridiculous nature of trivial Victorian concerns.

Algernon (Algy) Moncrieff

Algernon Moncrieff is a member of the wealthy class, living a life of total bachelorhood in a fashionable part of London. He is younger than Jack, takes less responsibility, and is always frivolous and irreverent. As a symbol, he is wittiness and aestheticism personified. He—like Jack—functions as a Victorian male with a life of deception. Unlike Jack, he is much more self-absorbed, allowing Wilde to discuss Victorian repression and guilt, which often result in narcissism.

Along with Lady Bracknell, Algy is given witty lines and epigrams showing his humor and disrespect for the society he will inherit. In discussing the music for Lady Bracknell's reception, Algernon says, "Of course the music is a great difficulty. You see, if one plays good music, people don't listen, and if one plays bad music, people don't talk." This is Algernon's wit and wisdom contained in a single line. Occasionally, he even congratulates himself on his humor: "It's perfectly phrased!" He poses and moves luxuriously about the stage with the studied languor of the aesthete who has nothing to do but admire his own wittiness. One might certainly see him as a representation of Wilde's cleverness and position in the aesthetic cult of the 1890s.

Parallel to Wilde in deception, Algernon is leading a double life. He uses an imaginary invalid friend, Bunbury, to get out of boring engagements and to provide excitement in the otherwise dull life of Victorian England. As he says, "A man who marries without knowing Bunbury has a very tedious time of it." This secrecy, of course, was also a facet of Wilde's life, which was unraveling before his Victorian audiences all too quickly by the time the play opened in London. With his irreverent attitudes about marrying and his propensity for a secret life, Algernon represents the rule-breaker side of Oscar Wilde—the side that eventually would meet its downfall in a notorious trial.

Finally, Algernon functions as an expression of the lengths to which Victorians had to go to escape the stifling moral repression and guilt brought about by a society that values appearance over reality. Algernon's constant references to eating and his repeated actions of gorging himself on cucumber sandwiches, muffins, and whatever food might be handy are symbols of total self-absorption, lust, and the physical pleasures denied by polite society. Just as institutions such as the church

(Chasuble) and the education system (Prism) function to keep people on the straight and narrow, human nature denies these restrictions and seems to have a will of its own. Algernon symbolizes the wild, unrestricted, curly-headed youngster who is happiest breaking the rules.

Lady Augusta Bracknell

The most memorable character and one who has a tremendous impact on the audience is Lady Augusta Bracknell. Wilde's audience would have identified most with her titled position and bearing. Wilde humorously makes her the tool of the conflict, and much of the satire. For the play to end as a comedy, her objections and obstacles must be dealt with and overcome.

Lady Bracknell is first and foremost a symbol of Victorian earnestness and the unhappiness it brings as a result. She is powerful, arrogant, ruthless to the extreme, conservative, and proper. In many ways, she represents Wilde's opinion of Victorian upper-class negativity, conservative and repressive values, and power.

Her opinions and mannerisms betray a careful and calculated speaking pattern. She is able to go round for round with the other characters on witty epigrams and social repartee. Despite her current position, Lady Bracknell was not always a member of the upper class; she was a social climber bent on marrying into the aristocracy. As a former member of the lower class, she represents the righteousness of the formerly excluded. Because she is now *Lady* Bracknell, she has opinions on society, marriage, religion, money, illness, death, and respectability. She is another of Wilde's inventions to present his satire on these subjects.

As a ruthless social climber and spokesperson for the status quo, Lady Bracknell's behavior enforces social discrimination and excludes those who do not fit into her new class. Her daughter's unsuitable marriage is an excellent example of how she flexes her muscles. She sees marriage as an alliance for property and social security; love or passion is not part of the mix. She bends the rules to suit her pleasure because she can. Jack will be placed on her list of eligible suitors only if he can pass her unpredictable and difficult test. She gives him ruthlessly "correct," but immoral, advice on his parents. "I would strongly advise you, Mr. Worthing, to try and acquire some relations as soon as possible, and to make a definite effort to produce at any rate one parent, of either sex, before the season is quite over." It matters not how Jack finds parent(s), just that he do it, following the requirements for acceptability.

Lady Bracknell's authority and power are extended over every character in the play. Her decision about the suitability of both marriages provides the conflict of the story. She tells her daughter quite explicitly, "Pardon me, you are not engaged to anyone. When you do become engaged to someone, I or your father, should his health permit him, will inform you of the fact." Done, decided, finished. She interrogates both Jack and Cecily, bribes Gwendolen's maid, and looks down her nose at both Chasuble and Prism.

Her social commentary on class structure is Wilde's commentary about how the privileged class of England keeps its power. Lady Bracknell firmly believes the middle and lower classes should never be taught to think or question. It would breed anarchy and the possibility that the upper class might lose its privileged position.

Wilde has created, with Augusta Bracknell, a memorable instrument of his satiric wit, questioning all he sees in Victorian upper-class society.

Gwendolen Fairfax & Cecily Cardew

Both Gwendolen Fairfax and Cecily Cardew provide Wilde with opportunities to discuss ideas and tout the New Woman near the turn of the century. They are curiously similar in many ways, but as the writer's tools, they have their differences.

Both women are smart, persistent and in pursuit of goals in which they take the initiative. Gwendolen follows Jack to the country—an atmosphere rather alien to her experiences, and Cecily pursues Algernon from the moment she lays eyes on him. Both women are perfectly capable of outwitting their jailers. Gwendolen escapes from her dominating mother, Lady Bracknell; Cecily outwits Jack by arranging for Algernon to stay, and she also manages to escape Miss Prism to carry on a tryst with her future fiancé. The first moment Cecily meets Algernon, she firmly explains her identity with a no-nonsense reaction to his patronizing comment.

For both women, appearances and style are important. Gwendolen must have the perfect proposal performed in the correct manner and must marry a man named Ernest simply because of the name's connotations. Cecily also craves appearance and style. She believes Jack's brother is a wicked man, and though she has never met such a man, she thinks the idea sounds romantic. She toys with rebelliously and romantically pursuing the "wicked brother," but she has full intentions of reforming him to the correct and appropriate appearance. The respectable name of Ernest for a husband is important to her. Both women, despite their differences, are products of a world in which how one does something is more important than why.

Cecily and Gwendolen are dissimilar in some aspects of their personalities and backgrounds. Gwendolen, on one hand, is confident, worldly, and at home in the big city of London. While her mother has taught her to be shortsighted like the lorgnette through which Gwendolen peers at the world, she has also brought her daughter up in a traditional family, the only such family in the entire play. On the other hand, Cecily is introduced in a garden setting, the child of a more sheltered, natural, and less-sophisticated environment. She has no mother figure other than the grim Miss Prism, and she has a guardian instead of a parent.

Gwendolen provides Wilde with the opportunity to discuss marriage, courtship and the absurdities of life. Her pronouncements on trivialities and her total contradictions of what she said two lines earlier make her the perfect instrument for Wilde to provide humor and to comment on inane Victorian attitudes. Cecily provides Wilde with an opportunity to discuss dull and boring education, Victorian values, money and security, and the repression of passion. More sheltered than Gwendolen, Cecily is still expected to learn her boring lessons and make a good marriage.

Both women seem ideally matched to their fiancés. Gwendolen is very no-nonsense and straightforward like Jack. She believes in appearances, upper-class snobbery, correct behavior, and the ability to discuss, ad nauseam, the trivial. Jack too is practical and takes his responsibilities quite seriously. While he has a sense of humor, he also realizes—especially in the country—that he must maintain a proper image and pay his bills. Cecily and Algernon are both guided by passion and immediate gratification. More emotional than their counterparts, they pursue life with a vengeance, aiming for what they desire and oblivious to the consequences. Both couples indulge in witty epigrams and are perfectly matched.

While Wilde spends most of his play satirizing Victorian ideals of courtship and marriage, he gets the last laugh with his female characters. Despite their positions in society as victims of the machinations of men, marriage contracts and property, the women are the strong characters who are firmly in control. Wilde provides two female characters who lack Lady Bracknell's ruthlessness, but who have the strength and practical sense that the men lack.

Rev. Chasuble & Miss Prism

These two comic and slightly grotesque caricatures are less developed than the principal players, and Wilde uses them to comment on religion and morality.

The minister is an intellectual character who speaks in metaphors. He is a "typical" country vicar who refers often to canon law and gives fatherly advice. Absent-mindedly in charge of his parishioners' souls, he performs christenings and interchangeable sermons, depending on the situation. Occasionally, however, his mask slips, and an interior world of lusty desire for Miss Prism appears. Often absent-minded, but always spouting moral platitudes, he symbolizes Wilde's view of Victorian religion and respectability.

Miss Prism is also intellectual, but in a literary way. She is a creative writer and a parody of "a woman with a past." She clearly had dreams of becoming a sensational romantic novelist, but, alas, she must make a living, so she is instead the jailer of Cecily and the guardian of her education and virtue. She, like the minister, makes constant moral judgments. Her favorite line, even to dead Ernest, is "As a man sows, so shall he reap." Repeating this often allows Wilde to show how meaningless and clichéd religion and values have become. As an instrument of the aristocracy, Miss Prism educates Cecily to conform to the dry, meaningless intellectual pursuits designed to keep the status quo. But, like Chasuble, beneath her surface she has a hedonistic streak; often her language slips when she ventures outside her Victorian appearance. She persists in inviting Chasuble to discuss marriage, pursues him diligently, and falls into his arms at the end.

Miss Prism is an appropriate character to uncover Jack's true history because she also is not what she seems. Wilde uses her to show what happens when dreams cannot be pursued in a society of strict social structure and stringent moral guidelines. Both she and Chasuble—with their lack of social opportunities—become servants to the system, promoting its continuation.

CRITICAL ESSAYS

On the pages that follow, the writer of this study guide provides critical scholarship on various aspects of Wilde's *The Importance of Being Earnest*. These interpretive essays are intended solely to enhance your understanding of the original literary work; they are supplemental materials and are not to replace your reading of *The Importance of Being Earnest*. When you're finished reading *The Importance of Being Earnest*, and prior to your reading this study guide's critical essays, consider making a bulleted list of what you think are the most important themes and symbols. Write a short paragraph under each bullet explaining *why* you think that theme or symbol is important; include at least one short quote from the original literary work that supports your contention. Then, test your list and reasons against those found in the following essays. Do you include themes and symbols that the study guide author doesn't? If so, this self test might indicate that you are well on your way to understanding original literary work. But if not, perhaps you will need to re-read *The Importance of Being Earnest*.

Duty and Respectability

The aristocratic Victorians valued duty and respectability above all else. *Earnestness*—a determined and serious desire to do the correct thing—was at the top of the code of conduct. Appearance was everything, and style was much more important than substance. So, while a person could lead a secret life, carry on affairs within marriage or have children outside of wedlock, society would look the other way as long as the appearance of propriety was maintained. For this reason, Wilde questions whether the more important or serious issues of the day are overlooked in favor of trivial concerns about appearance. Gwendolen is the paragon of this value. Her marriage proposal must be performed correctly, and her brother even practices correct proposals. Gwendolen's aristocratic attitude is "In matters of grave importance, style, not sincerity is the vital thing." The trivial is important; the serious is overlooked.

The tea ceremony in Act II is a hilarious example of Wilde's contention that manners and appearance are everything. The guise of correctness is the framework for war. Both women, thinking they are engaged to the same person, wage a civilized "war" over the tea service while the servants silently watch. When Gwendolen requests no sugar, Cecily adds four lumps to her cup. Although she asks for bread and butter, Gwendolen is given a large slice of cake. Her true feelings come out only in an aside that Cecily supposedly cannot hear: "Detestable girl!" Gwendolen is also appalled to find that Cecily is living in Jack's country home, and she inquires about a chaperone. Wilde gives examples again and again of the aristocrat's concern for propriety, that everything is done properly no matter what those good manners might be camouflaging.

The Absence of Compassion

Two areas in which the Victorians showed little sympathy or compassion were illness and death. When Lady Bracknell hears that Bunbury died after his doctors told him he could not live, she feels he has—in dying—acted appropriately because he had the correct medical advice. "Illness of any kind is hardly a thing to be encouraged in others. Health is the primary duty of life." Lady Bracknell, like other aristocrats, is too busy worrying about her own life, the advantages of her daughter's marriage, and her nephew's errors in judgment to feel any compassion for others. Gwendolen, learning from her mother, is totally self-absorbed and definite about what she wants. She tells Cecily, "I never travel without my diary. One should have something sensational to read in the train." Wilde seems to be taking to task a social class that thinks only of itself, showing little compassion or sympathy for the trials of those less fortunate.

Religion

Another serious subject—religion—is also a topic of satire. While concerns of the next world would be an appropriate topic for people of this world, it seems to be shoved aside in the Victorian era. Canon Chasuble is the symbol of religious thought, and Wilde uses him to show how little the Victorians concerned themselves with attitudes reflecting religious faith. Chasuble can rechristen, marry, bury, and encourage at a moment's notice with interchangeable sermons filled with meaningless platitudes. Even Lady Bracknell mentions that christenings are a waste of time and, especially, money. Chasuble's pious exterior betrays a racing pulse for Miss Prism: "Were I fortunate enough to be Miss Prism's pupil, I would hang upon her lips." Quickly correcting his error, the minister hides his hardly holy desires in the language of metaphor. Wilde's satire here is gentle and humorous, chiding a society for its self-importance.

Popular Culture

The popular attitudes of the day about the French, literary criticism, and books are also subjects of Wilde's humor. Wilde wittily asserts that Victorians believe that nothing good comes from France, except for (in Wilde's mind) the occasional lesbian maid. Otherwise, France is a good place to kill off and request the burial of Ernest. As the good reverend says, "I fear that hardly points to any very serious state of mind at the last." Literary criticism is for "people who haven't been at a University. They do it so well in the daily papers." Modern books are filled with truths that are never pure or simple, and scandalous books should be read but definitely in secret. Again Wilde criticizes the Victorians for believing that appearance is much more important than truth. He takes the opportunity to insert many examples of popular thought, revealing bias, social bigotry, thoughtlessness, and blind assumptions.

Secret Lives

Because Victorian norms were so repressive and suffocating, Wilde creates episodes in which his characters live secret lives or create false impressions to express who they really are. Jack and Algernon both create personas to be free. These other lives allow them to neglect their duties—in Algernon's case—or to leave their duties and pursue pleasure—in Jack's case. Very early in Act I, Wilde sets up these secret lives, and they follow through until the final act. When Jack and Algernon realize their marriages will end their pursuit of pleasure, they both admit rather earnestly, "You won't be able to run down to the country quite so often as you used to do, dear Algy," and "You won't be able to disappear to London quite so frequently as your wicked custom was." Marriage means the end of freedom, pleasure, wickedness, and the beginning of duty and doing what is expected. Of course, Jack and Algernon could continue to don their masks after they marry Gwendolen and Cecily, but they will have to be cautious and make sure society is looking the other way.

Passion and Morality

Wilde's contention that a whole world exists separate from Victorian manners and appearances is demonstrated in the girlish musings of Cecily. When she hears that Jack's "wicked" brother Ernest is around, she is intensely desirous of meeting him. She says to Algernon, "I hope you have not been leading a double life, pretending to be wicked and being really good all the time." The thought of meeting someone who lives outside the bounds of prudery and rules is exciting to naïve Cecily. Even using the name Ernest for his secret life is ironic because Algernon is not being dutiful—earnest—in living a secret life.

Various characters in the play allude to passion, sex, and moral looseness. Chasuble and Prism's flirting and coded conversations about things sexual, Algernon stuffing his face to satisfy his hungers, the diaries (which are the acceptable venues for passion), and Miss Prism's three-volume novel are all examples of an inner life covered up by suffocating rules. Even Algernon's aesthetic life of posing as the dandy, dressing with studied care, neglecting his bills, being unemployed, and pursuing pleasure instead of duty is an example of Victorians valuing trivialities. Once Algernon marries he will have suffocating rules and appearances to keep up. Wilde's characters allude to another life beneath the surface of Victorian correctness. Much of the humor in this play draws a fine line between the outer life of appearances and the inner life of rebellion against the social code that says life must be lived earnestly.

Courtship and Marriage

Oscar Wilde felt these Victorian values were perpetuated through courtship and marriage, both of which had their own rules and rituals. Marriage was a careful selection process. When Algernon explains that he plans to become engaged to Jack's ward, Cecily, Lady Bracknell decides, "I think some preliminary enquiry on my part would not be out of place." When Lady Bracknell pummels Jack with questions about parents, politics, fortune, addresses, expectations, family solicitors, and legal encumbrances, his answers must be proper and appropriate for a legal union between the two families to be approved. Fortune is especially important, and when Jack and Cecily's fortunes are both appropriate, the next problem is family background. Because Jack does not know his parents, Lady Bracknell suggests he find a parent—any with the right lineage will do—and find one quickly. Appearance, once again, is everything. Duty (not joy, love, or passion) is important, further substantiating Algy's contention that marriage is a loveless duty: "A man who marries without knowing Bunbury [an excuse for pleasure] has a very tedious time of it." Marriage is presented as a legal contract between consenting families of similar fortunes; background, love, and happiness have little to do with it.

Perpetuating the Upper Class

The strict Victorian class system, in which members of the same class marry each other, perpetuates the gulf between the upper, middle and lower classes. Snobbish, aristocratic attitudes further preserve the distance between these groups. Jack explains to Lady Bracknell that he has no politics. He considers himself a Liberal Unionist. Lady Bracknell finds his answer satisfactory because it means that he is a *Tory*, or a conservative. Jack's home in London is on the "unfashionable side" of Belgrave Square, so "that could easily be altered." When Jack inquires whether she means the "unfashionable" or the side of the street, Lady Bracknell explains, "Both, if necessary." The French Revolution is held up as an example of what happens when the lower class is taught to question its betters. Education is not for learning to think; it is for mindlessly following convention. Lady Bracknell approves of ignorance. In fact, she explains, "The whole theory of modern education is radically unsound. Fortunately in England, at any rate, education produces no effect whatsoever. If it did, it would prove a serious danger to the upper classes, and probably lead to acts of violence in Grosvenor Square." Thinking causes discontent, and discontent leads to social revolution. That simply will not do.

Class Conflict

One might think aristocrats would see the error of their ways and try to be more virtuous in a moral sense. However, they see their attitudes as the virtuous high ground and believe that other classes should conform to aristocratic attitudes and see the error of their own ways. When Miss Prism seems to chide the lower classes for producing so many children for Chasuble to christen, she appears to see it as a question of thrift. "I have often spoken to the poorer classes on the subject [of christenings]. But they don't seem to know what thrift is." Chasuble speaks humorously of the penchant of the aristocracy to dabble in good causes that do not disrupt their own lives too much. He mentions a sermon he gave for the Society for the Prevention of Discontent Among the Upper Orders. To the Victorians, reform means keeping the current social and economic system in place by perpetuating upper-class virtues and economy.

Every page, every line of dialogue, every character, each symbol, and every stage direction in *The Importance of Being Earnest* is bent on supporting Wilde's contention that social change happens as a matter of thoughtfulness. Art can bring about such thoughtfulness. If the eccentric or unusual is to be replaced with correct behavior and thought, human sympathy and compassion suffer. If strict moral values leave no room for question, a society loses much of what is known as humanity.

CliffsNotes Review

Use this CliffsNotes Review to test your understanding of the original text and reinforce what you've learned in this book. After you work through the review and essay questions, you're well on your way to understanding a comprehensive and meaningful interpretation of Oscar Wilde's *The Importance of Being Earnest*.

Q & A

1. Algernon is suspicious of Jack's personal life because he finds

   a. a letter to Jack from someone named Cecily

   b. a bill for a romantic dinner at Willis's

   c. a cigarette case with an inscription to Jack from an unknown woman

2. Jack wins Lady Bracknell's blessing for his marriage to Gwendolen by

   a. giving her a detailed written list of his finances

   b. threatening to remove his consent for Algernon's marriage to Cecily

   c. offering to name their first daughter Augusta

3. Jack makes up a story about his brother Ernest dying in

   a. Paris

   b. London

   c. Geneva

   d. Dublin

4. Both Algernon and Jack make an appointment with Dr. Chasuble to discuss

   a. their marriages

   b. their religious qualms

   c. their christenings

   d. their wedding vows

5. Cecily explains to Algernon that an engagement—to be serious—must be

   a. approved by her guardian

   b. broken at least once

   c. published in the London *Times*

   d. backed up by ready cash

6. Cecily and Gwendolen's conflict over their engagements is explored during

   a. tea time

   b. the christening of Ernest

   c. Mr. Gribsby's visit

   d. Reverend Chasuble's sermon

7. Lady Bracknell changes her mind about Cecily's suitability to marry Algernon when she learns of

   a. Jack's birth

   b. Cecily's education

   c. Algernon's latest escapade

   d. Cecily's fortune

8. The secret of Jack's birth and parentage is revealed through the past of

   a. Cecily

   b. Miss Prism

   c. Reverend Chasuble

   d. Gwendolen

Answers: (1) c. (2) b. (3) a. (4) c. (5) b. (6) a. (7) d. (8) b.

Identify the Quote: Find Each Quote in *The Importance of Being Earnest*

1. "A man who marries without knowing Bunbury has a very tedious time of it."

2. "The moment Algernon first mentioned to me that he had a friend called Ernest, I knew I was destined to love you."

3. "To be born, or at any rate, bred in a handbag, whether it had handles or not, seems to me to display a contempt for the ordinary decencies of family life that remind one of the worst excesses of the French Revolution."

4. "As a man sows, so let him reap."

5. "I am not in favour of long engagements. They give people the opportunity of finding out each other's character before marriage, which I think is never advisable."

6. "I've now realized for the first time in my life that Vital Importance of Being Earnest."

7. "All women become like their mothers. That is their tragedy. No man does. That's his."

8. "I have never met any really wicked person before. I feel rather frightened."

9. "I certainly wouldn't let Jack buy my outfit. He has no taste in neckties at all."

10. "Prism! Where is that baby?"

Answers: (1) Algernon (2) Gwendolen (3) Lady Bracknell (4) Miss Prism (5) Lady Bracknell (6) Jack (7) Algernon (8) Cecily (9) Algernon (10) Lady Bracknell

Essay Questions

1. Wilde's play has two settings—the city of London and the country. How does he create differences between the two settings?

2. What attitudes toward marriage do Wilde's characters explore?

3. How does Wilde create and comment on the differences between the social classes in England as represented by Lady Bracknell and the servants in both settings?

4. Manuscripts are used by various characters—diaries, sermons, and a three-volume novel. What function does each have in the play?

5. What attitudes of the aristocracy can be seen in Lady Bracknell's dialogue?

6. How is conflict developed in the play?

7. How does Wilde turn around well-known proverbs or epigrams to comment on Victorian attitudes?

Practice Projects

1. Research the Victorian period, and determine how accurate Wilde was in his assessment of the aristocratic attitudes of the period.

2. Design costumes that are historically accurate for each of the main characters in the play.

3. Research Wilde's opinions about politics and art. How do they apply to his play?

4. Design the stage sets for Wilde's play based on the stage directions, themes, and purposes of the play.

5. Using sources about the time period of the 1890s, draw a map that shows the various London locations mentioned in the play: Half-Moon Street, the Albany, Willis's, Grosvenor Square, Belgrave Square, the Empire, Upper Grosvenor Street, Bayswater, Gower Street, and Holloway Prison.

6. Join with others to act out a particular conversation between characters in one of the scenes.

7. Research the trials of Wilde near the end of his life. What do they reveal about the use of evidence? About justice? About how the courts viewed different social classes?

8. Research, compose, and act out an interview with Oscar Wilde. Include questions about Wilde's life, attitudes, and philosophy on art and beauty

CliffsNotes Resource Center

The learning doesn't need to stop here. The CliffsNotes Resource Center shows you the best of the best—links to the best information in print and online about the author and related works. And don't think that this book is all we've prepared for you; we've put all kinds of pertinent information at www.cliffsnotes.com. Look for the terrific resources at your favorite bookstore or local library and on the Internet. When you're online, make your first stop www.cliffsnotes.com, where you'll find more incredibly useful information about *The Importance of Being Earnest.*

Books

BECKSON, KARL. *Oscar Wilde: The Critical Heritage.* London: Routledge and Kegan Paul, 1970. This book discusses the early critical commentary on Wilde's works.

BIRD, ALAN. *The Plays of Oscar Wilde.* London: Vision Press, 1997. This book contains eight chapters about Wilde's plays with interesting comments on the metamorphoses of various versions of *Earnest.*

ELLMANN, RICHARD. *Oscar Wilde.* London: Hamish Hamilton, 1987. This is the most definitive biography written about Wilde.

HARRIS, FRANK. *Oscar Wilde: His Life and Confessions,* revised edition. London: Constable, 1938 (originally published in 1916). This book is very readable but not as complete or accurate as Ellmann's.

MILLER, ROBERT KEITH. *Oscar Wilde.* New York: Ungar, 1982. This book provides discussions of Wilde's plays. It is a useful and very readable biography.

POWELL, KERRY. *Oscar Wilde and the Theatre of the 1890s.* Cambridge: Cambridge University Press, 1990. This book describes the origins of the play, comments on themes, and discusses Ibsen's influence on Wilde.

RABY, PETER, ed. *The Cambridge Companion to Oscar Wilde.* Cambridge: Cambridge University Press, 1997. This book contains biographical material, places Wilde's work in perspective, discusses the confusion over Wilde's cause of death, comments on the play, and explains the background of British laws concerning homosexuality.

RABY, PETER. *Oscar Wilde.* Cambridge: Cambridge University Press, 1988. This book contains excellent commentary on Wilde's work by one of his strongest scholars.

SMALL, IAN. *Oscar Wilde Revalued.* Greensboro, NC: University of North Carolina Press, 1993. This is an excellent bibliography of works about Wilde with an appraisal of their worth during the many ages of Wilde criticism. It was number eight in the 1880–1920 British Author Series.

WORTH, KATHERINE. *Oscar Wilde.* London: Macmillan, 1983. This book discusses Wilde's life and comments on each act of the play.

Magazines and Journals

CRAFT, CHRISTOPHER. "Alias Bunbury: Desire and Termination in 'The Importance of Being Earnest,'" *Representations* 31 (1990): 19–46. This essay analyzes the sexuality in the play.

ELLMANN, RICHARD. "The Critic as Artist as Wilde," *Encounter* 29, 1 (1967): 28–37. Ellmann connects Wilde to early modernism.

GOPNIK, ADAM. "The Invention of Oscar Wilde," *The New Yorker* (May 18, 1998): 78–86. This article focuses on the life, personality, and family relationships of Wilde.

JAYS, DAVID. "Wilde Disappointment," *New Statesman* (September 25, 2000): 61–63. This article discusses paradoxes in Wilde's personality and life, and presents criticism of his works.

JOHNSON, WENDELL STACY. "Fallen Women, Lost Children: Wilde and the Theatre of the Nineties," *Tennessee Studies in Literature* 27 (1884): 196–211. This essay connects Wilde with contemporary theatre.

KENYON, KAREN. "Notable Britons: Oscar Wilde," *British Heritage* (April/May 2002): 12–14. This article discusses Wilde's biography and works.

ROBINS, ASHLEY and SEAN L. SELLARS. "Oscar Wilde's Terminal Illness; Reappraisal After a Century," *Lancet* (November 25, 2000): 1841–1843. This essay discusses the confusion over Wilde's cause of death, medical history, and diagnosis.

Internet

An Essay on Wilde, Society and Society Drama, http://www.english. upenn.edu/~cmazer/imp.html—This essay by Cary M. Mazer was prepared for a production of *Earnest* by People's Light and Theatre Company, Malvern, PA, June 1993. The essay describes 1890s theatre atmosphere, managers, audiences, the theatre district in London, clothing, actors, and the social context of Victorian times.

Costume Design, http://www.costumes.org/pages/earnest2.htm—
This site contains wonderful photos of costumes for an actual production at
Theatre University of Alaska Fairbanks Theatre Department. A great deal of
research is provided on costume design for *Earnest* (including corsets, starched
detachable collars, references to lines from the play concerning clothing, and
links to Victorian fashion pages). The site was researched, and the costumes
were designed by Tara Maginnis in 2000.

Importance of Being Earnest Site, http://www.eng.fju.edu.tw/
English_Literature/Earnest/Importance.html—This site con-
tains questions about each act and the play as a whole. Relevant links to Wilde,
the play, and Victorian society are included.

The Literature Network, http://www.online-literature.com/wilde/—
This site contains information on Wilde's life, the full text of *The Picture of
Dorian Gray*, *An Ideal Husband*, and *The Importance of Being Earnest*, as well
as short stories and poetry by Wilde.

The Victorian Web, http.//www.cyberartsweb.org/victorian/—This
is a huge Web site maintained by Brown University and filled with information about the Victorian Period. It has links to the play itself, pages on Oscar
Wilde, and sites on aesthetes and decadents.

Index

Made in the USA
San Bernardino, CA
04 February 2020